WHAT'S IT MADE OF?

WHAT'S IT MADE OF?

THE MATERIALS THAT SHAPE OUR WORLD

DK LONDON
Senior Editor Sam Kennedy
Senior Art Editor Stefan Podhorodecki
Managing Editor Francesca Baines
Managing Art Editor Philip Letsu
Production Editor Dragana Puvacic
Production Controller Joss Moore
Jacket Designer Stephanie Tan

DK DELHI
Senior Editor Neha Ruth Samuel
Project Art Editor Revati Anand
Project Editor Bipasha Roy
Editor Vandana Likhmania
Art Editor Prateek Maurya
Senior Picture Researcher Aditya Katyal
Rights and Permissions Specialist Vagisha Pushp
Deputy Manager, Picture Research Virien Chopra
Managing Editor Kingshuk Ghoshal
Managing Art Editor Govind Mittal
Pre-production Designer Anita Yadav
Pre-production Image Editor Vikram Singh
Creative Head Malavika Talukder

Publisher Andrew Macintyre
Art Director Mabel Chan

Authors Dr Kat Day, Clive Gifford, Hilary Lamb
Illustrators and Render Artists Max Kulich,
Simon Mumford, Aparajita Sen, Simon Tegg, Jack Williams
Consultant Dr Anna Ploszajski

First published in Great Britain in 2025 by
Dorling Kindersley Limited
20 Vauxhall Bridge Road,
London SW1V 2SA

The authorised representative in the EEA is
Dorling Kindersley Verlag GmbH. Arnulfstr. 124,
80636 Munich, Germany

Copyright © 2025 Dorling Kindersley Limited
A Penguin Random House Company
10 9 8 7 6 5 4 3 2 1
001–341861–Oct/2025

All rights reserved.
No part of this publication may be reproduced, stored in or introduced into a retrieval system, or transmitted, in any form, or by any means (electronic, mechanical, photocopying, recording, or otherwise), without the prior written permission of the copyright owner.

DK values and supports copyright. Thank you for respecting intellectual property laws by not reproducing, scanning or distributing any part of this publication by any means without permission. By purchasing an authorised edition, you are supporting writers and artists and enabling DK to continue to publish books that inform and inspire readers. No part of this publication may be used or reproduced in any manner for the purpose of training artificial intelligence technologies or systems. In accordance with Article 4(3) of the DSM Directive 2019/790, DK expressly reserves this work from the text and data mining exception.

A CIP catalogue record for this book
is available from the British Library.
ISBN: 978-0-2416-8315-6

Printed and bound in China

www.dk.com

CONTENTS

Our material world 6

CHAPTER 1
IN YOUR BAG

Headphones	10
Using aluminium	12
Ballpoint pen	14
Quartz watch	16
Using sand	18
Artificial skin	20
Smartphone	22
Using lithium	24
Lithium fields	26
Using polyester	28
Inside sun cream	30
Using silicon	32
Money	34

CHAPTER 2
PLAY

Running shoes	38
Using silver	40
Football boots	42
Using rubber	44
Gaming handset	46
Using polyethylene	48
Glowstick	50
Bowling ball	52
Paints in art	54
Gecko tape	56
Electric guitar	58
Using wood	60
Upright piano	62
Drum kit	64
Using fabric	66
Using diamonds	68

CHAPTER 3
HOME

Striking a match	72
Fire retardant	74
Electric toaster	76
Microwave oven	78
Packaging	80
Using copper	82
Washing machine	84
Soap bubble	86
Fridge freezer	88
Clay pottery	90
Using ceramics	92
Toothpaste	94
Using wool	96

CHAPTER 4
OUT AND ABOUT

Skiing	100
Using water	102
Hybrid SUV car	104
Car airbag	106
Mountain bike	108
Using glass	110
Binoculars	112
Using petroleum	114
Jet airliner	116
Fire extinguisher	118
Using cement and concrete	120
Ship lock	122
3D printer	124
3D-printed steel bridge	126
Using steel	128
Mars rover Curiosity	130
Spacesuit	132

REFERENCE

Using gold	134
Metals and alloys	138
Carbon materials	140
Noble gases	141
Glass, ceramics, and concrete	142
Natural materials	144
Synthetic polymers	146
Composite materials	148
Recycling and sustainability	150

Glossary	152
Index	154
Acknowledgments	158

OUR MATERIAL WORLD

Everything is made from materials. Every object you use – from a wooden chair to a metallic toaster – has been thoughtfully designed and crafted from raw materials into a finished product.

PROBLEM TO SOLVE
Product development begins with a problem. For instance, the need for a cheaper, easier way to get from A to B.

PROCESSING MATERIALS
Materials may come from the ground, from plants, or from animals. Then they must be processed into a usable, safe form. Processing involves anything from heating to treating with chemicals.

PRODUCT IDEA
A bicycle solves the problem! But now designers must answer more questions. Is the bike for smooth or rough surfaces? How fast does it need to go? The answers help them decide which materials to use.

MATERIALS SELECTION
All materials have different properties that designers must weigh up. A bicycle with an aluminium frame would be cheap and lightweight, good for road riding. A mountain bike would benefit from a more shock-resistant titanium frame.

RECYCLED MATERIALS
Recycling materials is cheaper and requires less energy than extracting new raw materials from the Earth. Today, many companies make products from recycled materials. A bicycle might make use of a frame of recycled metal and tyres of recycled rubber.

HANDMADE PRODUCTS
Not all products are manufactured in factories. Some items are entirely handmade by skilled craftspeople. The result is often something bespoke (designed for the individual customer). This process is more labour intensive, but the craftsperson has the skill and experience to make the most of the material's unique qualities.

OUR MATERIAL WORLD | 7

MANUFACTURING

Once the materials have been obtained, the bicycle can be built. At this point some materials go through an intermediate stage, to change their properties using heat, or to mix them together to create a final composite material.

DISTRIBUTION

To get the bicycle to the final user, many other products and materials are used. This ranges from steel shipping containers, to the recycled paper used in cardboard packaging.

USING THE PRODUCT

Ready to go!

Finally, the bicycle reaches the user. If it is well designed with the right materials for the job it should keep working for a long time. But even when an object no longer functions, the materials in it don't disappear. They can be re-used to make a new product or, if necessary, disposed of.

REUSE

Bicycles and many other products can be broken up into reusable parts. These can be used in a new bicycle, or as something entirely different.

LANDFILL

Products and parts that cannot be reused go to landfill sites. But even here people can find and reclaim useful materials that were thrown away.

CHAPTER 1
IN YOUR BAG

IN YOUR BAG | 11

HEADPHONES

Headphones are a pair of small loudspeakers worn over the ears. They allow music or other audio to be listened to by a single person. Headphones convert an electric signal to vibrations, using an electromagnet to control a thin sheet of material called a diaphragm that moves back and forth rapidly, producing sound.

HOW DOES IT WORK?

Headphones speakers work by converting electrical signals into vibrations. When electrical current goes through the voice coil, it produces an electromagnetic field. The now-magnetic voice coil then continuously attracts and repels the permanent magnet, causing it to vibrate. This pushes a diaphragm up and down, generating sound waves.

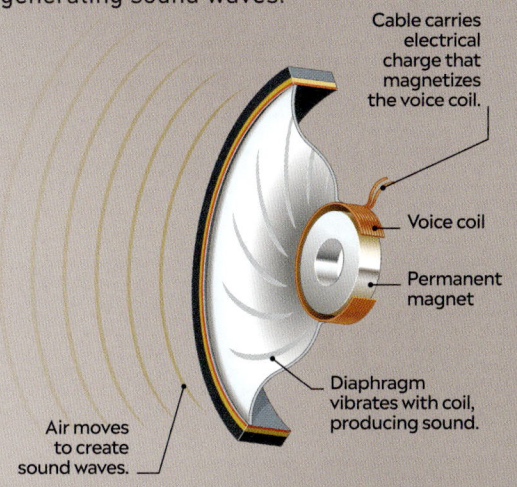

Cable carries electrical charge that magnetizes the voice coil.

Voice coil

Permanent magnet

Diaphragm vibrates with coil, producing sound.

Air moves to create sound waves.

NEODYMIUM MAGNET
Powerful and permanent

These are extremely strong permanent magnets made from neodymium (right), iron, and boron. In headphone speakers, they interact with the electromagnetic field generated by the voice coil to create vibrations that help produce sound.

Copper
Copper is an excellent electrical conductor, making it suitable for carrying the electrical current that generates a magnetic field around the voice coil.

Aluminium
Aluminium is a relatively lightweight but strong metal, making the headphones comfortable to wear for hours at a time.

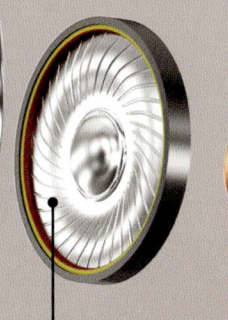

BERYLLIUM
Lightweight and conductive

Beryllium is a soft metal with good electrical conductivity and a strong resistance to corrosion. It is used in some high-end headphones to make the vibrating diaphragm.

Electronics controlling the headphones are printed and fixed on a circuit board, usually made of fibreglass.

12 | IN YOUR BAG

USING ALUMINIUM

The metal aluminium is the third most common element in Earth's crust, and must be unlocked from rocky ores, such as bauxite. It is a resilient, easily workable, and versatile metal that is used to construct everything from sporting goods to spacecraft.

ELECTRICAL DEVICES

Lightweight frames of laptops and the bodies of many electrical appliances are formed from aluminium.

WINDOW FRAMES

Corrosion-resistant window frames are made from aluminium, which can be easily cut and shaped.

POWER LINES

Light and cheap aluminium cable conducts electricity well.

HOW IS IT EXTRACTED?

Bauxite ore is mined, crushed, and processed to create a compound called aluminium oxide, or alumina. Aluminium is extracted from this alumina using powerful electrical currents in a process called electrolysis. Any impurities left are skimmed off the molten metal inside a foundry.

Bauxite mining

Removing impurities from aluminium

GOLF CLUBS

BICYCLE FRAMES

Tubing made of an aluminium alloy is welded together to create a light but sturdy frame.

PURE ALUMINIUM
Soft metal

Soft and delicate in its pure state, aluminium is alloyed with small amounts of substances such as copper and lithium to make it stronger and more useful. Around 75 per cent of all aluminium produced is still in use because we keep recycling it.

IN YOUR BAG   13

More than 420 billion lightweight aluminium drinks cans are produced each year.

ALUMINIUM CANS

Food packaging is often made of aluminium foil, which is not toxic.

FOOD CONTAINER

ALUMINIUM FOIL
Aluminium is the world's second most malleable metal, after gold. It can be rolled into thin sheets known as foils. Some foils are a mere 0.006 mm (0.0002 in) in thickness.

Foil wrapping repels water and keeps heat inside this vent pipe.

THERMAL INSULATION

AIRCRAFT FRAME

This robotic helicopter is made of aluminium and carbon fibre.

INGENUITY, MARS HELICOPTER

Door panels and other car parts are formed from aluminium sheets.

Aluminium is used to make lighter trains that require less fuel to move faster.

TRAIN BODY

CAR BODYWORK

ALUMINIUM MAKES UP ABOUT 8.2% OF EARTH'S CRUST.

BALLPOINT PEN

A ballpoint pen dispenses oil-based ink over a small, smooth ball placed at its tip. As you write, ink is transferred to the paper as the ball rolls over it. Ballpoint pens are the most commonly used writing instruments in the world today.

A BALLPOINT PEN HOLDS ENOUGH INK TO DRAW A LINE ABOUT 2 KM (1.25 MILES) LONG.

Resin in ink acts as a binder, helping the ink stick to paper and dry quickly.

PIGMENT
Creating colour

Pigments are powders that add colour to the ink. In the past, pigments were made from natural materials such as minerals and plants. Most pigments used today, such as the deep Prussian blue, are made from chemicals.

TUNGSTEN CARBIDE
Harder than steel

A compound of carbon and the metal tungsten, tungsten carbide is used to make the ball of the pen. This tough material protects the tip from wear and tear. It also provides a smooth surface so the ink can be distributed evenly.

IN YOUR BAG | 15

OLEIC ACID
Smooth motion

Oleic acid, a common fatty acid found in vegetable oils such as olive oil (right), is added to the ink as a lubricant. It helps the ball roll smoothly over paper.

HOW DOES IT WORK?

To make a mark on paper, the ball of the pen must be pressed on the paper's surface, pushing it up towards the ink chamber behind it. As the ball rotates, it picks up ink from the chamber and deposits it on the paper. Then the resin hardens, protecting the pigment in the ink from smudging.

Long chamber of ink sits just behind the ball.

Ball dips into the ink chamber when pressed against the paper.

Writing with a ballpoint pen

The ink spreads evenly because it contains a chemical called alkyl alkanolamide, which reduces friction between the ball and the paper.

The ink contains benzyl alcohol, a solvent that helps dissolve the pigment.

Body made from stainless steel

16 | IN YOUR BAG

QUARTZ WATCH

The introduction of quartz into watches in 1969 revolutionized the time-keeping industry. Watches no longer needed to be wound daily and kept time much more accurately. Purely mechanical watches could lose up to 10 seconds a day, but adding a quartz crystal powered by a battery reduced this lag to as little as 15 seconds a year.

Plexiglass
This flexible, transparent plastic is strong and shatter-proof, which means it won't break if the watch is dropped or knocked. Also known as PMMA, it is made in sheets and can be moulded into any shape when hot.

QUARTZ IS THE SECOND MOST ABUNDANT MINERAL IN EARTH'S CRUST.

STRONTIUM
Long-lasting luminescence

This soft, silvery-yellow metal is often used as a key ingredient in glow-in-the-dark features because of its long-lasting phosphorescence (ability to absorb light energy and emit it later).

HOW DOES IT WORK?

A tiny quartz crystal is at the heart of the watch. When an electric current passes through the crystal, it resonates (vibrates) at a precise frequency of 32,768 times a second. A microchip counts these vibrations and sends an electrical signal to the watch's stepper motor to move the hands of the watch at exactly one tick per second.

Housed inside a cylindrical casing, the quartz crystal's vibrations are turned into regular electric pulses, one per second.

Motor turns gears that sweep hands around the clockface to keep time.

Battery provides current to microchip circuit.

Electric pulses drive miniature electric stepper motor.

Brushed chrome
Giving the bracelet a brushed chrome finish produces a less shiny, matte appearance.

IN YOUR BAG

NATURAL SAND
Crafted by nature
Rocks and stones are gradually weathered or eroded by wind, waves, rainfall, and ice until they break down into tiny pieces. This process can take many thousands of years.

MORTAR

Sand filters trap dirt particles.

WATER FILTRATION

BRICKS

When added to paints, sand creates a grainy surface with a lot of grip.

PAINTS

Sand accounts for a large proportion of the ingredients used to make glass.

GLASS

USING SAND

Loose pieces of rocks and particles of minerals, all smaller than gravel but larger than silt, make up sand. This natural material is a key ingredient in construction - it is mixed with clay to form bricks, used to make mortar, and combined with cement and gravel to form concrete.

SOME 50 BILLION TONNES OF SAND AND GRAVEL ARE USED EACH YEAR.

IN YOUR BAG | 19

THE DEMAND FOR SAND IS PROJECTED TO RISE BY 45% IN THE NEXT 40 YEARS.

SILICON WAFER

Silicon extracted from sand is used in microprocessors and other microchips that run electronic devices.

Fine sand is mixed with water and lime or gypsum to form a smooth paste called plaster, which is applied to walls to protect them from damage.

PLASTERING

Typical concrete mixtures contain twice as much sand as cement.

CONCRETE

Sand and water fired with compressed air removes paint or rust from surfaces.

SANDBLASTING

M SAND
Artificial sand

Manufactured sand, or M sand, is made by mechanically grinding down rocks. It is free of silt and clay, and has even-sized particles that may have either a fine or a coarse texture. This sand is mainly used for construction.

HOW IS SAND EXTRACTED?

Natural sand is obtained from quarries, ocean beds, or beaches. It is filtered into similarly sized pieces, then cleaned and stored for use. Its composition is shaped by the kinds of rocks and minerals carried to the region by wind or water, and how these are broken down.

Open pit quarries
Most natural sand is extracted from giant holes or quarries dug into the ground. It is then sent to a facility for processing so that it can be made suitable for use.

Ocean beds
Machines known as dredgers extract sand from the ocean floor, river beds and estuaries, where rivers meet the sea.

Beaches and dunes
Small-scale mining of beaches for sand is common, but it is illegal in some areas as the removal of sand can damage coastal ecosystems.

ARTIFICIAL SKIN

Scientists have developed artificial skin that can replace human skin affected by injuries, disease, or burns. It is usually made with biological materials such as human skin cells and collagen (a protein), and is sometimes combined with synthetic polymers such as silicone. Lab-grown synthetic skin can prevent the spread of infections and help damaged skin heal itself.

IN YOUR BAG

LITHIUM
Electrical powerhouse

Electrically-charged lithium atoms, called ions, flow between the battery's anode (positive) and cathode (negative) terminals to help generate the flow of electric current that powers the phone.

Lepidolite
Lithium is often extracted from this mineral to make phone batteries.

Camera module contains an LED flash for illuminating dark scenes.

Copper
As a good electrical conductor, copper is used for flexible ribbon cables that connect different circuit boards inside the phone.

Carbon fibre-reinforced plastic
Adding carbon fibre to plastic makes the outer casing tough but lightweight.

Nickel
A thin coating of this metal shields the circuits from any radio interference.

TUNGSTEN
Vibrating weight

A small amount of this very dense metal is used to make an unbalanced weight at one end of the vibrating motor (left). As the motor spins, the weight at the end turns and, because it spins off centre, the phone moves fractionally back and forth – the vibration.

Silicon
Cheap to source and easy to work with, silicon is often used to make the microprocessors that control smartphones, as well as the memory chips that store large amounts of data.

IN YOUR BAG | 23

INDIUM TIN OXIDE
Touchscreen film

This material is transparent and conducts electricity well, so it is used to make a thin film that lies between layers of glass in the phone screen. It allows your fingers to complete an electric circuit when they touch, swipe, or pinch the screen.

Silver
About 0.5 g (0.02 oz) of this rare metal is found in phones, mostly as connections between components.

Glass
Aluminosilicate glass with added potassium ions forms a thin, scratch- and shatter-resistant glass screen.

Aluminium
This metal creates a strong, light frame.

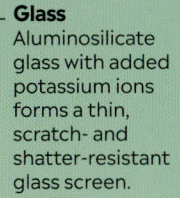

Gold
Minute amounts are used in the electrical contacts of a SIM card.

SMARTPHONE

Smartphones are marvels of miniaturization. More than 300 tiny parts, plus a rechargeable battery, are all crammed inside their slimline cases. Working together, the components give you all the computing power of a 1990s supercomputer inside a lightweight device you can slip into your pocket.

24 | IN YOUR BAG

A typical electric car's batteries contain around 8 kg (17.6 lbs) of lithium.

ELECTRIC CAR

LITHIUM-ION BATTERIES

Lithium is used in rechargeable batteries, which power computers and smartphones, and in non-rechargeable batteries inside some clocks and pacemakers.

ELECTRIC BIKE

SMARTPHONE

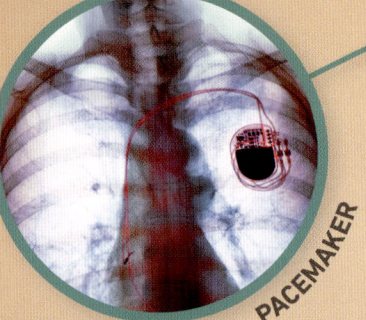

PACEMAKER

Lithium-ion batteries are small, but can power a device for a long time.

LITHIUM
Reactive metal

Lithium is obtained through mining solid deposits or evaporating lithium-rich waters. It reacts easily with water and oxygen in its pure form, so it has to be processed into compounds, such as lithium salts, for storage and use.

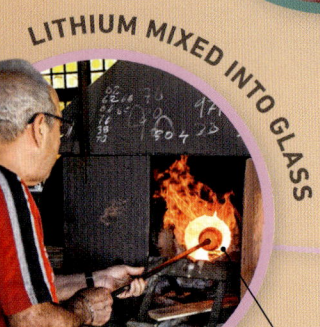

LITHIUM MIXED INTO GLASS

Lithium oxide lowers the melting point of glass.

LITHIUM OXIDES

Compounds of lithium and oxygen are used in glass-making, ceramic glazes, and industrial cooling systems to reduce corrosion.

USING LITHIUM

Five times lighter than aluminium and fourteen times lighter than iron, this silvery, soft metal has the lowest density of any solid element. It helps power the world as a key component in rechargeable batteries.

INDUSTRIAL COOLING TOWER

CERAMIC GLAZE

IN YOUR BAG 25

OVER 50% OF THE WORLD'S LITHIUM IS MINED IN SOUTH AMERICA.

The entire frame of this helicopter is made of aluminium-lithium alloy.

HELICOPTER FRAME

LITHIUM ALLOYS

Adding lithium to other metals can create lightweight alloys with great strength and stiffness. Aluminium-lithium alloys, for example, are used widely in making parts of jet engines.

Aluminium-lithium powder strengthens this baseball bat.

BASEBALL BAT

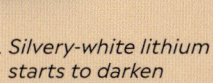

Silvery-white lithium starts to darken when exposed to air.

Brakes made of lithium alloy are heat resistant and can withstand high temperatures.

RACING CAR BRAKES

MEDICINE

OTHER LITHIUM COMPOUNDS

Lithium is combined with various substances to produce valuable chemicals such as lithium carbonate, which is processed in this plant in Bolivia.

Lithium carbonate drugs act as anti-depressants and mood stabilizers.

RED FIREWORKS

AIR CONDITIONING COOLANTS

Fireworks containing lithium carbonate burn with a rich red colour.

Lithium bromide solution is used as a coolant and air dryer in air conditioners.

LITHIUM FIELDS

Most of the lithium needed for lithium-ion batteries is extracted from these colourful pools in the Salar de Atacama salt flats in Chile. The pools are formed by pumping out the salt-rich water beneath the flats. As the water evaporates, the colours change from pale turquoise to canary yellow until all that is left is the dry lithium salts.

IN YOUR BAG

USING POLYESTER

The word "polyester" refers to a family of plastics that are mostly made from crude oil. Polyester fibres can form fabrics that are waterproof, windproof, and wrinkle-resistant. The first polyester fabric, Terylene®, was launched in 1941.

POLYCARBONATE
Impact-resistant plastic
This type of polyester material is stiff, hard, and tough. Polycarbonates are often used as an alternative to glass as well as in DVDs and car dashboards.

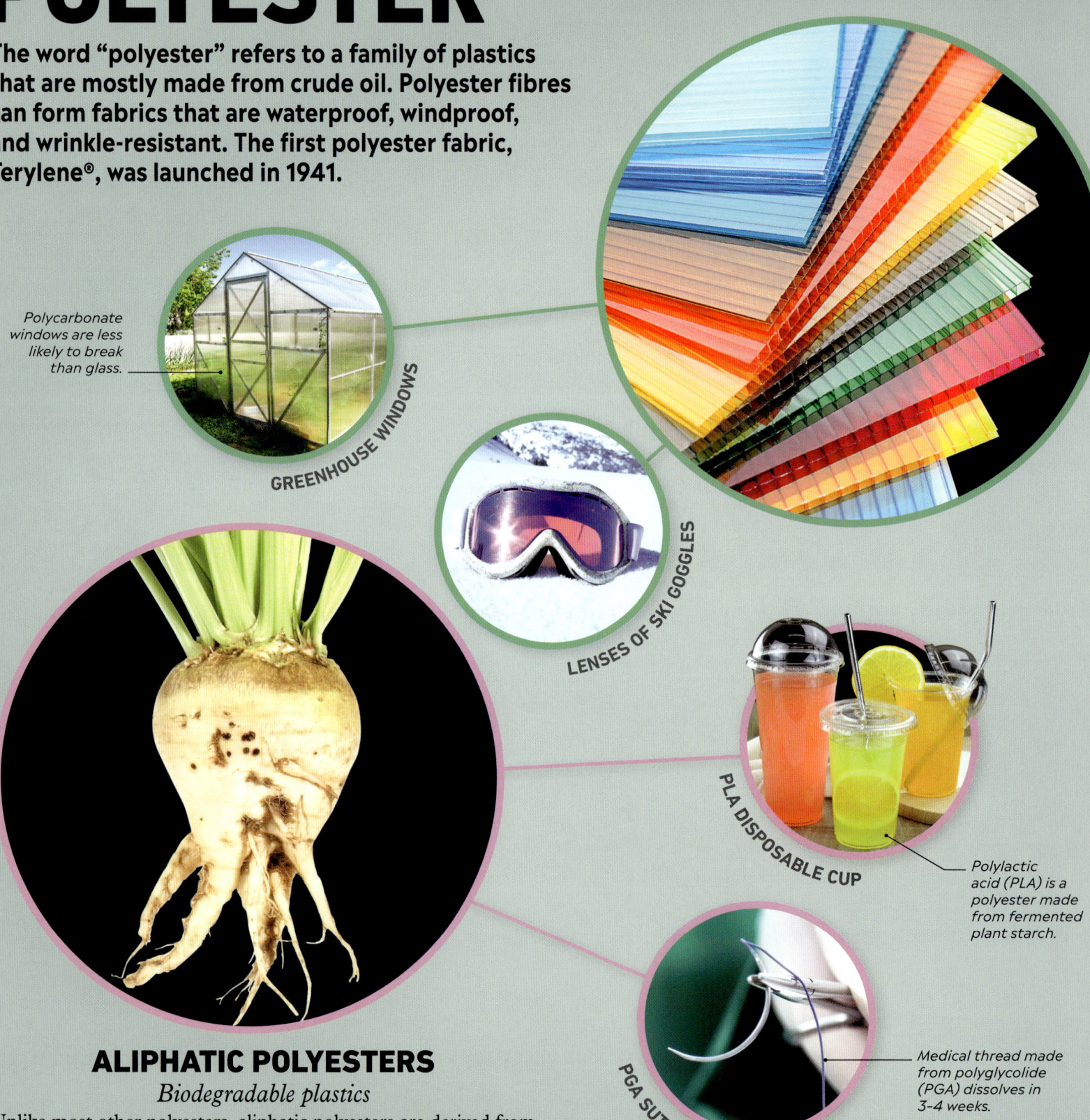

Polycarbonate windows are less likely to break than glass.

GREENHOUSE WINDOWS

LENSES OF SKI GOGGLES

PLA DISPOSABLE CUP

Polylactic acid (PLA) is a polyester made from fermented plant starch.

PGA SUTURE THREAD

Medical thread made from polyglycolide (PGA) dissolves in 3–4 weeks.

ALIPHATIC POLYESTERS
Biodegradable plastics
Unlike most other polyesters, aliphatic polyesters are derived from plants such as this sugar beet and other natural products. As a result, they rot after use more quickly than oil-based plastics.

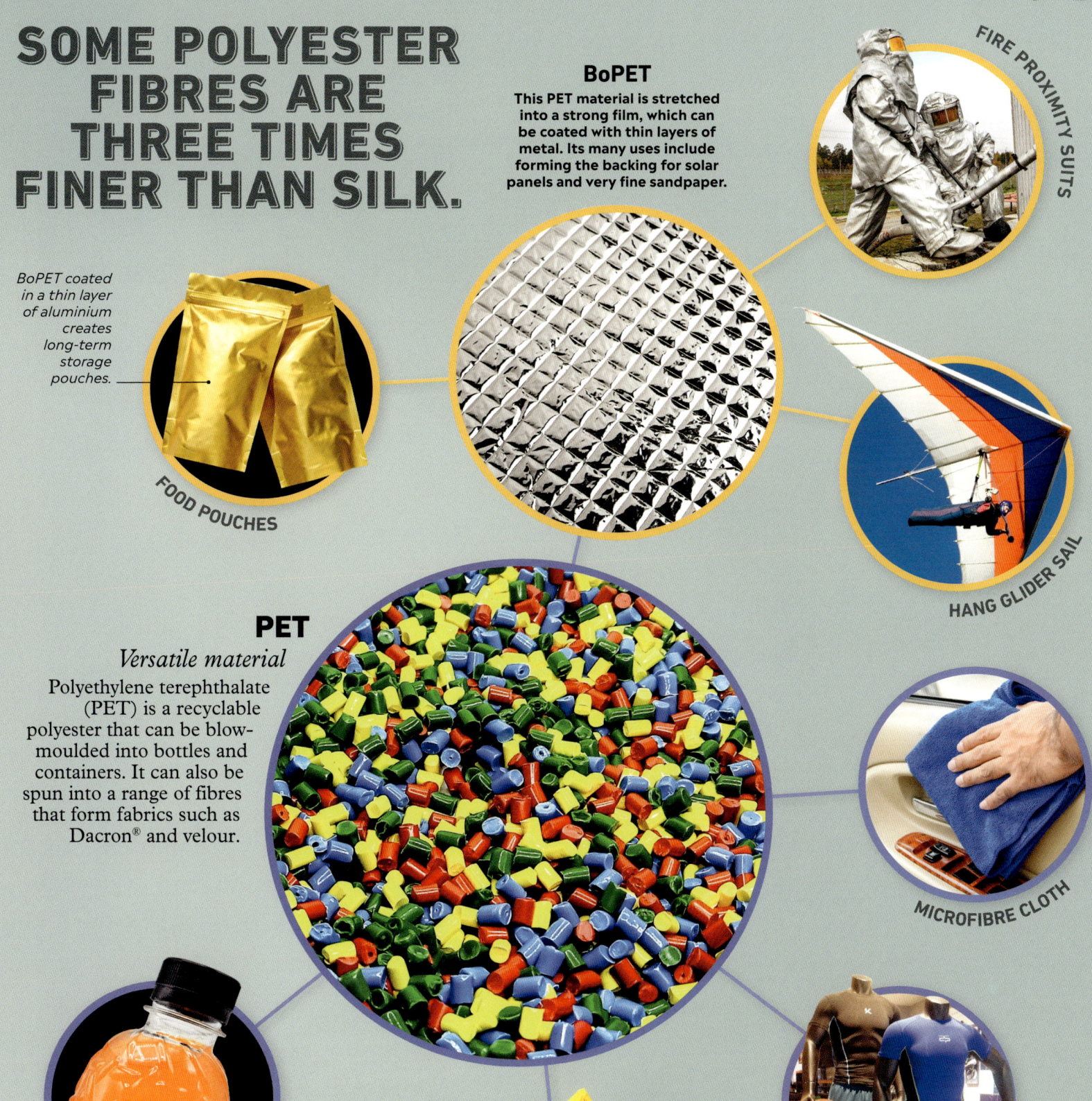

SOME POLYESTER FIBRES ARE THREE TIMES FINER THAN SILK.

BoPET

This PET material is stretched into a strong film, which can be coated with thin layers of metal. Its many uses include forming the backing for solar panels and very fine sandpaper.

FIRE PROXIMITY SUITS

BoPET coated in a thin layer of aluminium creates long-term storage pouches.

FOOD POUCHES

HANG GLIDER SAIL

PET

Versatile material

Polyethylene terephthalate (PET) is a recyclable polyester that can be blow-moulded into bottles and containers. It can also be spun into a range of fibres that form fabrics such as Dacron® and velour.

MICROFIBRE CLOTH

PLASTIC BOTTLES

A third of all PET produced goes into making disposable plastic bottles.

RAIN COAT

GYM WEAR

INSIDE SUN CREAM

This image (magnified 1000x) of a blob of sun cream shows a silicone microsphere. This is a microscopic particle of silicone, a synthetic polymer made of silicon, oxygen, hydrogen, and carbon. These microspheres serve two purposes. They scatter light and absorb excess oil, making the cream less sticky.

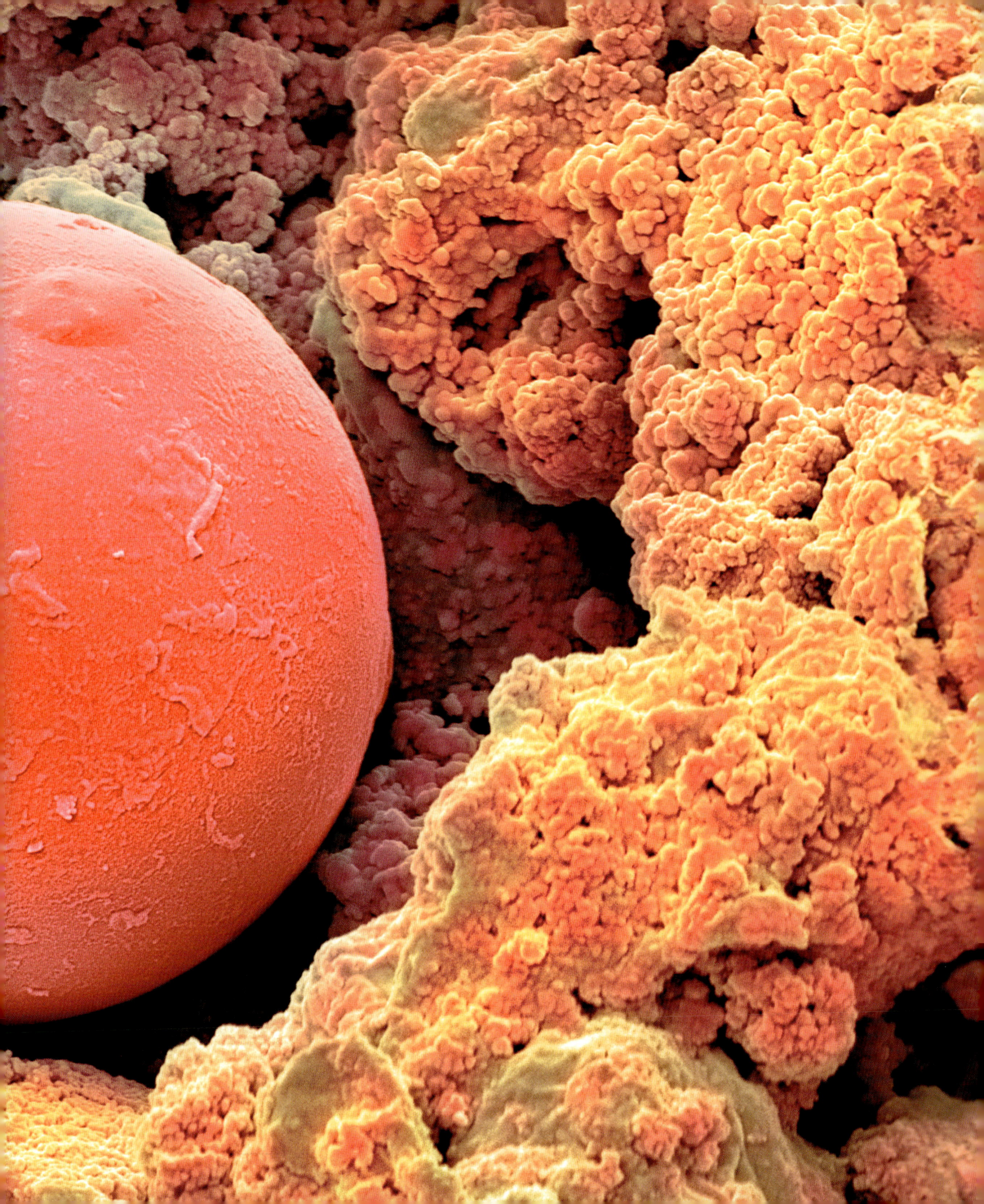

IN YOUR BAG

SILICON MELTS AT A SEARING 1,414°C (2,577°F).

JEWELLERY

Synthetic moissanite – gemstone made of silicon carbide – reflects light almost as well as natural diamonds.

SILICON CARBIDE
Also known as carborundum, silicon carbide is a hard compound of silicon and carbon often used as an abrasive (a coarse material to polish tough surfaces). It is also used in electronic devices as a semiconductor – a material that conducts electricity or insulates against it based on the temperature or the applied electrical current.

SILUMIN

Metals can be welded together using wire made from silumin, a silicon-aluminium alloy.

KNIFE SHARPENING

Silicon makes an excellent semiconductor and helps convert sunlight into electricity in solar panels.

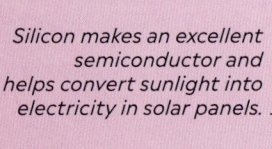

SOLAR PANEL

USING SILICON

Silicon is very reactive, so it is not seen in its pure form on Earth. Instead it is found as a compound in the rocks and minerals of our planet's crust. It has applications in construction, renewable energy, and electronics.

PURE SILICON
Crystalline substance

Silicon is a hard, crystalline solid that looks like – but is not – a metal. It makes up 27.7 per cent of Earth's crust. It has to be extracted from silicon dioxide (silica) or silicates (compounds with other elements such as aluminium).

SILICON WAFER

The silicon used to make microchips needs to be 99.9999999 per cent pure. A silicon wafer contains dozens of microprocessors each etched with microscopic circuits.

IN YOUR BAG | 33

PORCELAIN VASE
Porcelain is made from sand, which contains about 95 per cent silica.

PORTLAND CEMENT

ANTI-CAKING AGENT
Silica is added to powdered foods to prevent them clumping and binding together.

SILICA AEROGEL
This insulator of heat is one of the lightest known solid materials.

GLASS MAKING

SILICA
This compound of silicon and oxygen is a strong, glassy material that makes an excellent insulator. It is a key ingredient in glass, cement, and concrete, and in many tyres. Silica gel is used as a drying agent.

COOKWARE

SEALANT
Silicone dries and hardens to form a waterproof seal between tiles.

GASKETS
Silicone O-rings are durable and flexible, forming robust seals between different parts of an object.

TOYS

SILICONE
This rubbery polymer is made up of silicon, carbon, hydrogen, and oxygen. It is widely used as a special liquid and grease, and as a flexible, mouldable solid. Silicone is often more resistant to high temperatures than other rubber materials.

UV-FLUORESCENT INK
Glowing print

The ultraviolet (UV) numbers found on some banknotes are printed with UV-fluorescent ink. This ink absorbs UV light and emits visible light, causing it to "glow" under a UV light. This is important in checking for forgeries.

Serial numbers are printed on every banknote for identification.

Tiny letters that can be read with a magnifying glass are printed along the bottom.

Unique geometric patterns on Euro notes prevent modern photocopiers from making copies.

Cotton paper
Euro notes are printed on paper made from cotton. This is more durable than paper made from wood.

THE EAGLE FEATURES ON MORE THAN 40 CURRENCIES AROUND THE WORLD.

HOW A SECURITY THREAD WORKS

A security thread is a thin ribbon of metal or plastic woven into a bank note. It is an important security feature, typically containing tiny, hard-to-copy features such as holograms and microprinting of features so small they cannot be seen with the naked eye.

MONEY

Money comes in many physical forms, including banknotes made of paper or polymer. In addition to detailed images, these notes often incorporate security features such as holograms, foil patches, fluorescent markings, raised print, and see-through windows – all of which aim to make the notes difficult to forge.

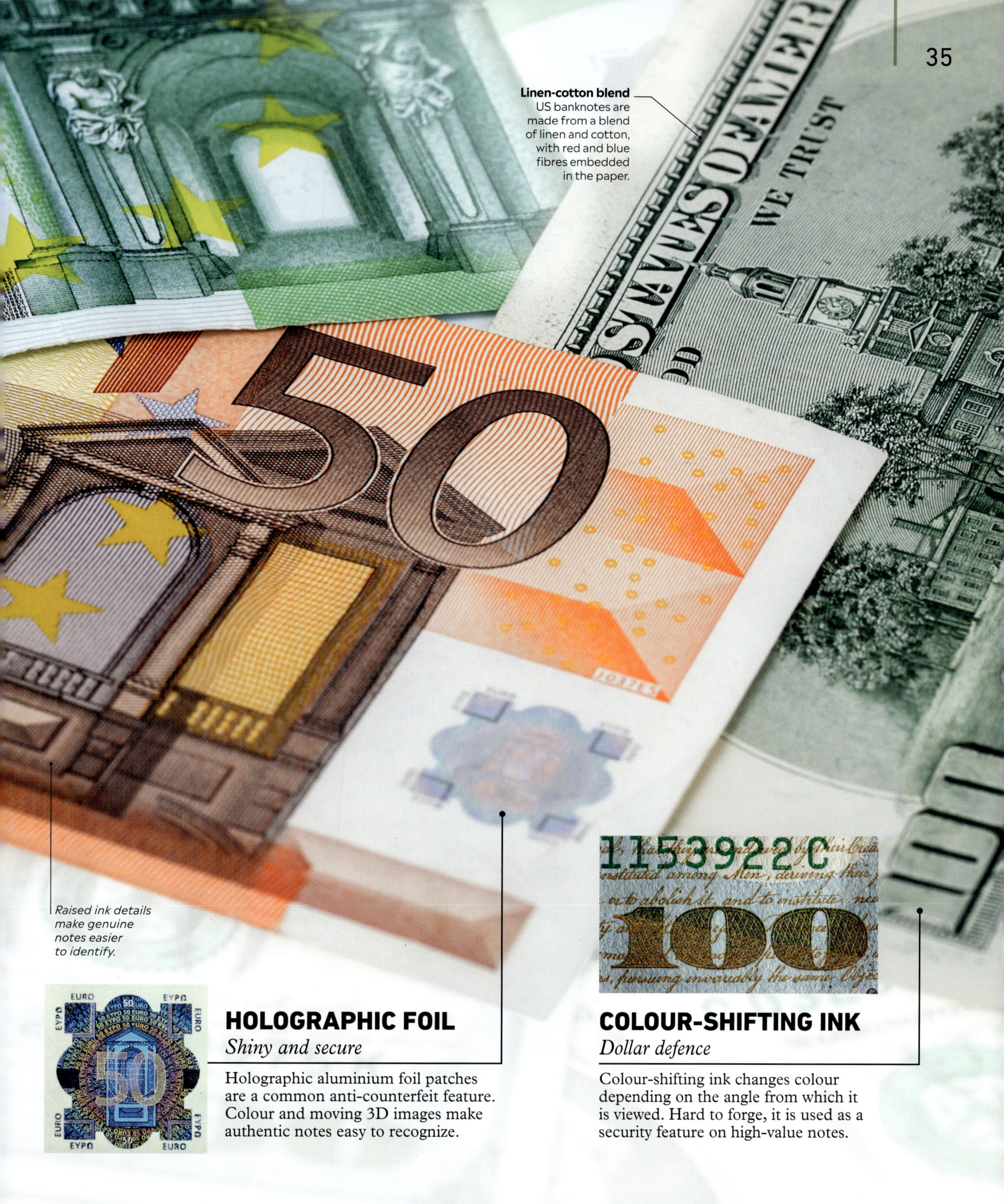

Linen-cotton blend
US banknotes are made from a blend of linen and cotton, with red and blue fibres embedded in the paper.

Raised ink details make genuine notes easier to identify.

HOLOGRAPHIC FOIL
Shiny and secure

Holographic aluminium foil patches are a common anti-counterfeit feature. Colour and moving 3D images make authentic notes easy to recognize.

COLOUR-SHIFTING INK
Dollar defence

Colour-shifting ink changes colour depending on the angle from which it is viewed. Hard to forge, it is used as a security feature on high-value notes.

CHAPTER 2
PLAY

PLAY

RUNNING SHOES

Running shoes are designed with high-performance features such as textured rubber soles for gripping the ground and foam midsoles that absorb shock. To keep them comfortable to wear for long periods of time, running shoes make use of several lightweight, flexible, breathable materials.

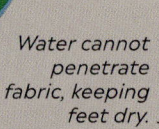

Collar supports the wearer's ankle.

Polyester
The upper mesh is made of durable plastic perforated with lots of tiny holes to draw moisture away from the foot.

Water cannot penetrate fabric, keeping feet dry.

RECYCLING PLASTIC

Many clothing manufacturers use a percentage of recycled materials in their products. This allows plastic waste to be turned into new – often very different – products.

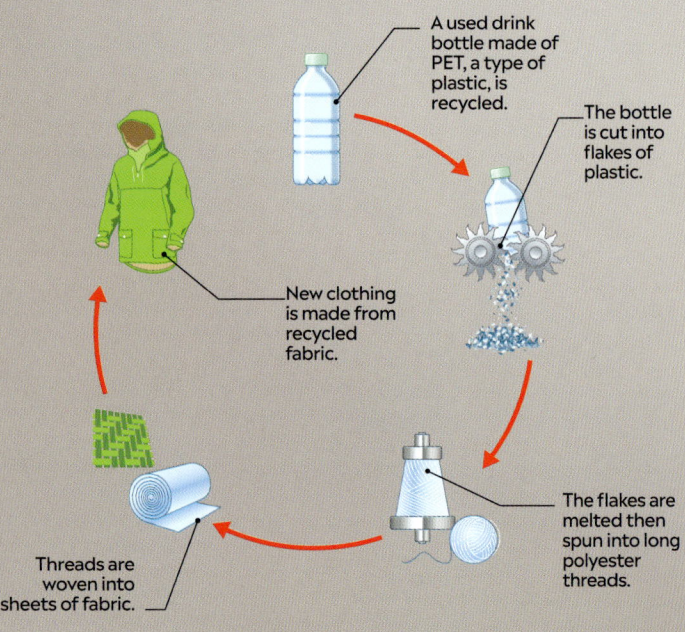

A used drink bottle made of PET, a type of plastic, is recycled.

The bottle is cut into flakes of plastic.

The flakes are melted then spun into long polyester threads.

Threads are woven into sheets of fabric.

New clothing is made from recycled fabric.

LAMINATED FABRIC
Tough textiles

This composite material is made by sticking together layers of two or more different fabrics. This results in a product that combines the properties of all the individual fabrics. In running shoes, laminated fabric is usually made from woven layers to be light, strong, and water-resistant.

"Eyestay" lace loop is resistant to tearing under strain from the laces.

Plastic
Moulded plastic outer layer helps trainers keep their shape.

SILVER
Stink buster

Silver nanoparticles are used to coat sportswear textiles as they can kill the bacteria responsible for producing odour. Silver nanoparticles are also found in wound dressings and antimicrobial creams, and can be used to disinfect water.

Shock-absorbing insole made from "spongy" plastic foam.

Additional cushioning in heel

EVA FOAM
Midsoles

Synthetic ethylene vinyl acetate (EVA) plastic foam is filled with air, making it durable but very lightweight, a good thermal insulator, and highly shock-absorbent. It is an ideal midsole material, keeping the foot warm and absorbing impacts that could otherwise cause injuries.

EVA foam is comprised of minuscule cells containing air.

Rubber
Waterproof and grippy, rubber is ideal for the shoe's sole.

USING SILVER

The precious metal silver is an excellent conductor of heat and electricity. This versatile material has many uses in industry – its compounds can act as a catalyst to speed up chemical reactions, make special sunglasses darken in bright light, and put the snap-bang in Christmas crackers.

MIRRORS
The polished silver surface of a mirror can reflect up to 95 per cent of the light that hits it.

SILVER BULLION BARS

SILVER HALIDES IN X-RAY
A plastic film coated with the compound silver halide is used to develop X-ray images.

ANTIBACTERIAL CREAM
Silver sulfadiazine (SSD) is an antibiotic used on burns to prevent infection.

SILVER IN MEDICINE
This metal has strong antimicrobial properties. Silver and its compounds are added to antiseptic creams and wound dressings to kill fungi and bacteria responsible for infections, moulds, and odours. Silver particles in sportswear prevent the growth of bacteria due to sweat.

NANOPARTICLES IN SPORTS CLOTHING

WATER PURIFICATION
Silver ions added to drinking water help purify it in space.

SOLID SILVER
Soft, shiny metal

Silver is a whitish, lustrous metal. It is sometimes found in its pure form, but is generally processed from ore. Most silver production today involves extracting the metal from gold, copper, and lead ores.

PLAY | 41

OLD SILVER COINS

JEWELLERY

Hallmark stamp provides proof of purity and quality of silver.

SILVERWARE

STERLING SILVER
Pure silver is often alloyed with other metals to make it stronger, harder, and more durable. Sterling silver is a popular alloy which contains 92.5 per cent silver and 7.5 per cent of another metal, such as copper.

Silver is printed onto membrane switches found in circuits for keypads like this.

MEMBRANE SWITCHES

Silver solder is used to join electronic components to a circuit board.

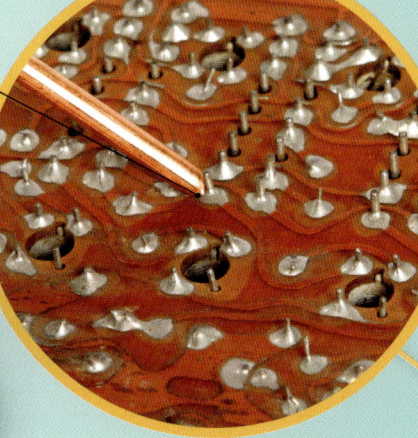

SILVER IN ELECTRONICS
Among the metallic elements, silver is the best conductor of electricity. It is used to fuse electrical components to circuit boards and to make the connectors and switches found in many devices, including computer keyboards, mobile phones, and TVs.

Silver paste within photovoltaic cells helps carry the produced electricity away.

SOLAR CELLS

SILVER THREADS

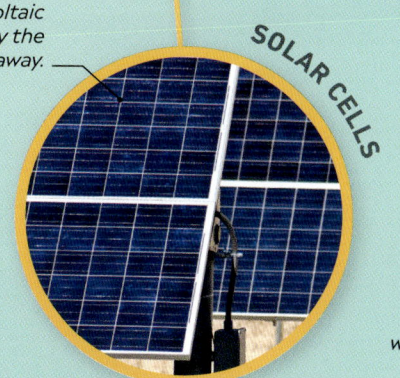

Touchscreen gloves have silver threads that let the wearer use the smartphone without taking them off.

SILVER IODIDE IS USED TO MAKE CLOUDS PRODUCE RAIN.

PLAY

FOOTBALL BOOTS

The first football boots were designed in the 19th century. They were made of thick leather, with metal nails sticking out of the sole for better grip. Modern football boots are made of lightweight, flexible, and durable materials, and are much more comfortable to wear than their ancestors.

THE EARLIEST FOOTBALL BOOTS WEIGHED ABOUT 500 G (1.1 LBS).

Polyester
Socks made of polyester dry quickly after absorbing sweat.

Shoelaces are generally made from cotton or polyester, which do not fray easily.

LEATHER
Flexible fabric

Most football shoes are made of leather (below), synthetic materials, such as polyurethane, or both. Leather moulds to the foot and takes its shape easily. Leather boots are also flexible, durable, and breathable.

PLAY | 43

TPU
Thermoplastic polyurethane (TPU) is a durable plastic often used to make the outsole (outermost layer of the sole) because it resists scratches and cracks.

TYPES OF FOOTBALL SHOE

Different football boots are used on different playing surfaces. Shoes with metal studs are useful on damp or muddy grass pitches as they reduce slippages and falls when a player is running. Rubber or plastic moulded studs help players make quick turns on firm, dry grounds. Boots with rubber lugs (bumps) are used on slippery artificial turfs as metal studs can get caught in synthetic grass. Flat rubber soles provide the best grip on smooth indoor wooden floors.

Metal studs

Moulded studs

Small rubber lugs

Flat rubber sole

Foam layers inside the boot protect and support the feet.

ALUMINIUM
Durable metal

When playing on soft ground, shoes with metal studs provide players with better grip by digging into the turf. The studs are generally made of aluminium alloys, which do not wear or break easily.

44 | PLAY
USING RUBBER

Few families of materials are more elastic than bendy, stretchy rubbers. It is found in two forms, natural and synthetic. Both are strong, mouldable, and extremely flexible. Rubber is also waterproof, a good electrical insulator, and resistant to many corrosive substances.

MOTOR VEHICLE TYRES
2.4 billion motor vehicle tyres are manufactured every year. Both natural and synthetic rubber can be used to make tyres strong, durable, and shock-absorbent, ensuring a comfortable ride.

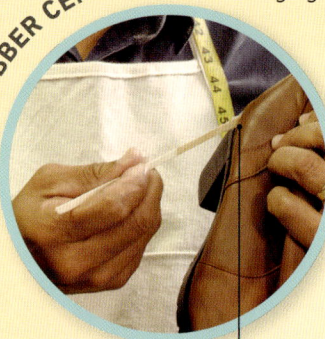

RUBBER CEMENT

Often used in handicrafts and shoe repairs, rubber cement can glue leather, paper, card, and rubber.

Rubber sheets hanging out to dry

UNCURED RUBBER
Raw natural rubber that has not been chemically treated (known as uncured) is a soft material that can deform. It is also quite sticky, making it useful in adhesives.

RUBBER BANDS

LATEX GLOVES

CURED RUBBER
Natural rubber is heated with sulphur compounds and other chemicals to improve its durability, strength, and flexibility. This chemically treated rubber has a wide range of uses, from footwear and toys to hoses and conveyor belts.

NATURAL RUBBER
Stretchy substance

Natural rubber is made from latex, a milky, white sap extracted from the trunks of *Hevea brasiliensis* trees. A single tree produces 60-150 kg (132-330 lbs) of latex during its lifetime.

PLAY 45

Rubber crumb granules made by shredding old tyres are added to asphalt to reduce road noise.

RUBBER CRUMB

SPORTS PITCH

Running tracks, playgrounds, and some tennis courts feature rubber crumb surfaces.

RECYCLED RUBBER
Old tyres are recycled to make floor tiles and mats, roofing materials, bins, and many more everyday items. Recycling is an eco-friendly way of dealing with tyre waste and reduces the demand for new natural rubber, which helps preserve resources.

Wetsuit made of a form of rubber called neoprene acts as a barrier against cold water.

WETSUIT

SHREDDED RUBBER

Shredded tyres are used in landfill rubbish sites to improve drainage.

BALLOONS

LANDSCAPING

In gardens, shredded rubber can suppress the growth of weeds.

SHOE SOLES

SYNTHETIC RUBBER
Industrially made rubber

Originally created to meet the increasing demands for natural rubber, synthetic rubber now has many industrial uses due to its greater resistance to heat and oils. It is made from chemicals derived from coal or crude oil.

AROUND 70% OF THE WORLD'S NATURAL RUBBER IS USED IN TYRES.

46 | PLAY

Polycarbonate
Buttons are typically made of this tough and versatile thermoplastic.

The control stick is usually made of the same thermoplastic as the buttons.

These coverings secure the potentiometers and protect them from wear.

The plastic is moulded to fit comfortably in the player's hands.

ABS
Tough, smooth surface

The controller's outer casing is made from acrylonitrile butadiene styrene (ABS), a type of thermoplastic. ABS pellets are melted and then moulded into a smoothly contoured shape that is comfortable for players to hold for many hours at a time.

GRAPHITE
Electrical conductor

The movements of the control stick are turned into electrical signals by potentiometers (position sensors). These devices usually contain graphite, a soft form of carbon that conducts electricity well.

GAMING HANDSET

Modern controllers are designed to make games feel more interactive and immersive. They are made of plastic that is comfortable to hold and makes the controller feel like an extension of the hand. Concealed electronics track movement and provide vibrations and haptic feedback (the sense of "touch" when interacting with virtual objects).

PLAY | 47

HOW DOES IT WORK?

Most modern controllers include Voice Coil Motors that make the handset vibrate in sync with the game. A current passing through a coil of wire generates a magnetic field that interacts with another magnetic field produced by a permanent magnet. This causes the permanent magnet to move rapidly back and forth – to vibrate.

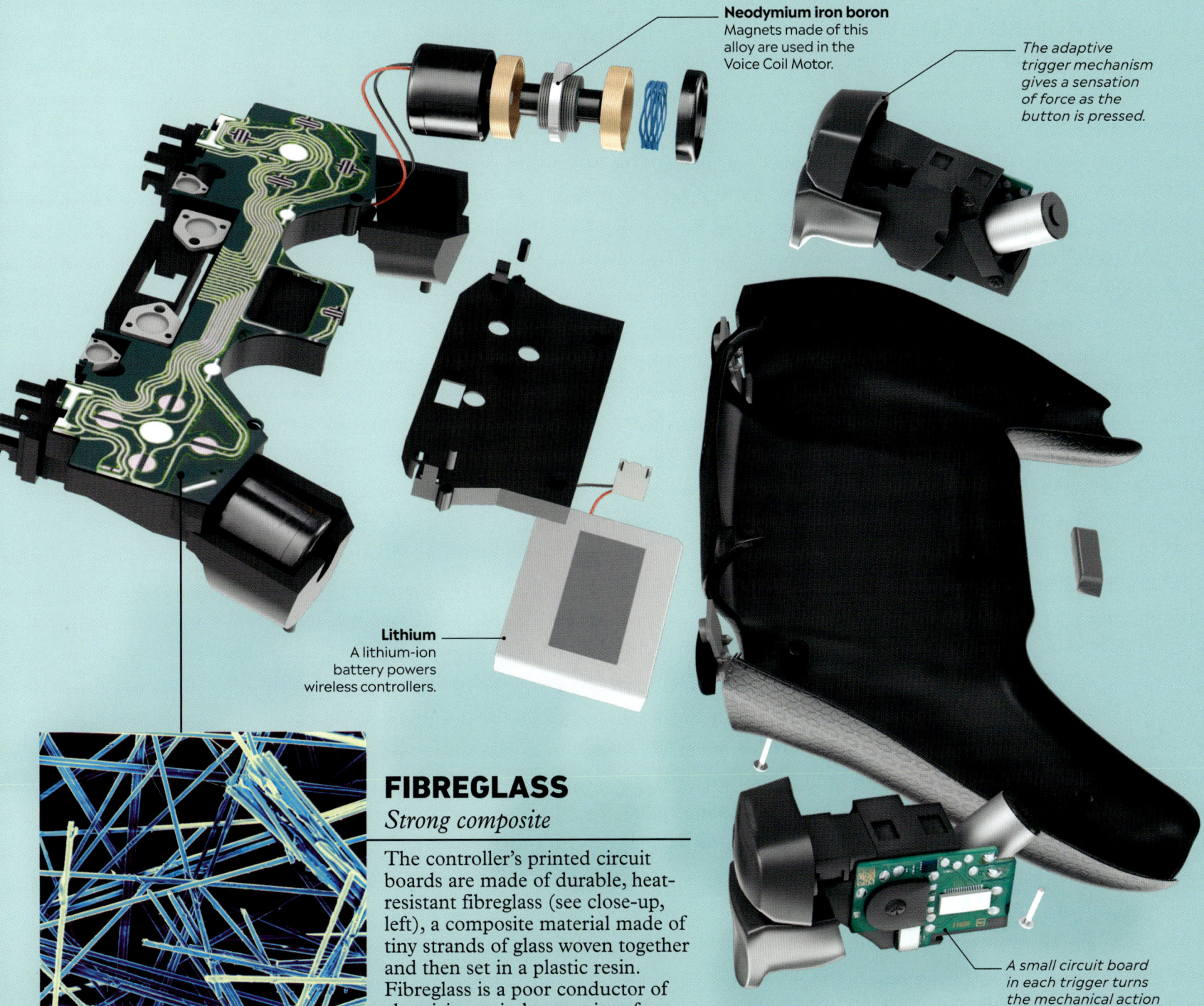

Copper coil conducts the electrical current that generates the magnetic field.

A yoke on either side of the permanent magnet helps shape the magnetic field.

Shaft restricts the movement of the magnet to a single back and forth direction.

Permanent magnet moves to create the vibrations.

Wavespring cushions the magnet from bumping into the coil's edges.

Neodymium iron boron
Magnets made of this alloy are used in the Voice Coil Motor.

The adaptive trigger mechanism gives a sensation of force as the button is pressed.

Lithium
A lithium-ion battery powers wireless controllers.

FIBREGLASS
Strong composite

The controller's printed circuit boards are made of durable, heat-resistant fibreglass (see close-up, left), a composite material made of tiny strands of glass woven together and then set in a plastic resin. Fibreglass is a poor conductor of electricity, so it does not interfere with the circuit board's wiring.

A small circuit board in each trigger turns the mechanical action of pulling the trigger into electrical signals reflected in the game.

USING POLYETHYLENE

This tough, flexible type of plastic is very versatile – it is used for lightweight food packaging and shopping bags as well as hardwearing tubes for plumbing. Polyethylene makes up a third of all plastics produced around the world, and can also be recycled to create new products.

SAFETY HELMETS

HDPE
Stronger than LDPE but not as stretchable, high-density polyethylene (HDPE) is formed into sheets or moulded into many sturdy products, including bins, crates, and outdoor furniture.

Outdoor bins are made using HDPE, which is sturdy and resistant to rotting.

PLUMBING

RECYCLING BINS

MDPE
Medium-density polyethylene (MDPE) is stronger than LDPE and more flexible than HDPE. It is used in outside plumbing, storage tanks, and playground plastics.

PLAYGROUND SLIDE

SQUEEZY BOTTLE

ETHYLENE PLANT
Plastic from oil
Ethylene is a compound obtained from crude oil and gas. Different processes are used to change these raw materials into the various forms of polyethylene.

PLAY | 49

POLYETHYLENE CAN BE RECYCLED AND REUSED.

WIRE COATINGS

PLASTIC BAGS

BUBBLE WRAP

Food packages, such as bread bags, are made from LLDPE film.

FOOD PACKAGING

LDPE
Low-density polyethylene (LDPE) is lightweight and very flexible, making it great for bags and bin liners.

LLDPE
Linear low-density polyethylene (LLDPE) is lighter and more flexible than LDPE. It is used for making toys and in packaging as film and shrink wrap.

TOYS

Toys made from LLDPE are non-toxic and safe for toddlers to chew on.

UHMWPE tiles form the surface of ice hockey rinks.

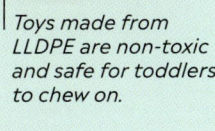

SURFACE BOARD OF ICE HOCKEY RINK

UHMWPE
Ultra-high-molecular-weight polyethylene (UHMWPE) is tough and stiff but difficult to shape. It is used to make objects that need to be very robust, such as floating jetties in harbours.

GEARS

BODY ARMOUR PANELS

Bullet-proof vests use UHMWPE panels for their high strength and light weight.

GLOWSTICK

A glowstick produces light through a chemical reaction called chemiluminescence. Often used for fun at parties, glowsticks give off light but no heat, and they don't need electricity or fire to ignite. However, they can only be used once and after they're activated they last for just a few hours.

Glass
The capsule inside the flexible plastic tube is brittle and easy to break under pressure.

Screw cap is factory sealed so chemicals cannot escape.

HOW DOES IT WORK?

Inside a glowstick is a glass capsule containing hydrogen peroxide. Bending the stick breaks the capsule, allowing hydrogen peroxide to mix with oxalate ester and produce a chemical that releases energy. This energy is transferred to the dye, which causes the dye to glow as it releases visible light.

Unused stick
Chemicals are separated, with hydrogen peroxide in glass container.

Bent stick
Bending the flexible plastic stick breaks the glass, allowing chemicals to mix.

Activated stick
Mixed chemicals react together, causing the fluorescent dye to emit light.

Plastic
The outer tube is made of flexible plastic that snaps back into position after being bent.

WHAT MAKES THE DIFFERENT COLOURS?

The chemical reaction in the tube transfers energy to the fluorescent dye, causing it to glow a certain colour. The colour of the light depends on the dye's chemical structure, with different dyes releasing light at different visible wavelengths.

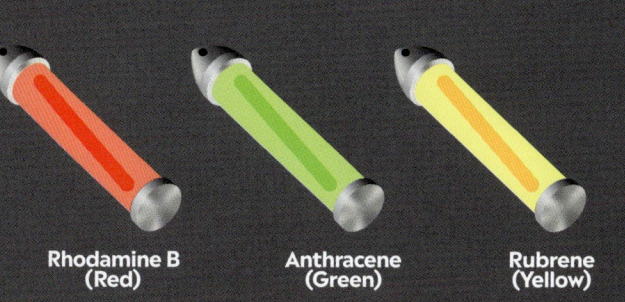

Rhodamine B (Red) Anthracene (Green) Rubrene (Yellow)

A hook on the end of the tube makes it easy to attach the glowstick to a bag or item of clothing.

PHENYL OXALATE ESTER
Getting glowing

The plastic tube holds a solution of an organic compound called phenyl oxalate ester and a fluorescent dye. Mixing the oxalate ester with hydrogen peroxide solution causes an oxidation reaction. This produces an unstable chemical that causes the dye to fluoresce (emit light).

Sodium salicylate
This chemical inside the tube acts as a catalyst, making the dye in the stick glow faster and brighter.

52 | PLAY

INNER CORE
Dynamic engine

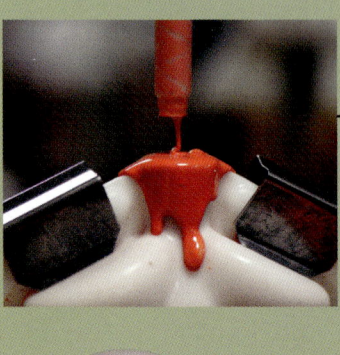

Also known as a "weight block", the central core determines the ball's motion. It can be made from ceramic or liquid polyester resin (plastic) with heavy metal oxides, limestone, or graphite added.

Pins in bowling alleys always have a pair of red stripes painted around the neck.

BISMUTH
Heavy metal

A powdered oxide of this metal is a popular choice for adding weight to the inner core due to its high density and low melting point (for pouring into moulds). In its pure form, bismuth has a silvery-pink crystalline structure.

The outer core is added to make the whole core spherical. It is made from a much lighter blend of polyester resin than the inner core.

The inner core determines how the ball spins and curves as it rolls. Professional balls have shapes designed to make the ball curl in towards the bowling pins.

Some professional balls have a reactive urethane veneer, which has microscopic holes to give the ball more grip.

PLAY | 53

Nylon
Each bowling pin is coated in a protective layer of nylon. This hardwearing and versatile plastic is used because it has some elasticity, which means it won't crack easily.

The pin is made from straight pieces of wood, glued and pressed together, then shaped.

Each pin must be the same weight, so sections are often cut out to meet the regulation standard.

ROCK MAPLE
To take the knocks

Ten-pin bowling pins take plenty of high-impact knocks from heavy bowling balls, so rock maple is chosen because of its strength and durability. Its straight grain also allows it to be shaped easily.

HOW DOES IT WORK?

Bowling balls are made of three layers: the inner core, the outer core, and a veneer. The layers are created in stages, with each layer of resin being poured into a mould in turn. Ball manufacturers zealously guard their secret recipes for the blend of ingredients they use in each resin layer.

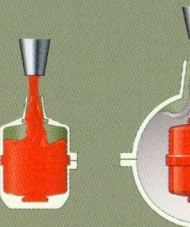  

1. The hot resin is poured into the core mould. It is ready to be extracted in two minutes.

2. The inner core is placed inside another mould and the blend for the outer core is poured in.

3. After two days, a third mould is used to add the final layer of shiny, outer resin for the veneer.

OUTER SHELL OR VENEER
Protective coating

A bowling ball's outer layer, also known as its "coverstock", is made from polyurethane – a synthetic resin with some elasticity, like rubber. Once the shell is solidified, it is either polished or sanded for higher friction.

BOWLING BALL

Early ten-pin bowling balls were made of wood, then hard rubber. Today, ten-pin bowling is played by 120 million people worldwide, most of whom play the game for fun, but there are those who play it as a professional sport. This has turned bowling ball design into a science, with "high-spec" cores and outer shells to alter the ball's trajectory.

PAINTS IN ART

Paints are substances used to create marks on a surface. There are many types of paint available today, such as oil paints, acrylics, and watercolours. They may use natural or synthetic materials but they all contain pigments for colour and binders that help them stick to surfaces.

THE OLDEST KNOWN CAVE PAINTING IS ABOUT 50,000 YEARS OLD.

MEDIEVAL PAINTS

Before the invention of synthetic paints, artists mostly relied on natural pigments, such as carmine red made from crushed insects and ultramarine from lapis lazuli. These were mixed with water and egg yolk to create tempera paints that spread easily and dried quickly.

Tempera gives the painting a matte finish.

Gold leaf detail

Triptych of the Madonna and Child with Saints by Neri Di Bicci, 1440

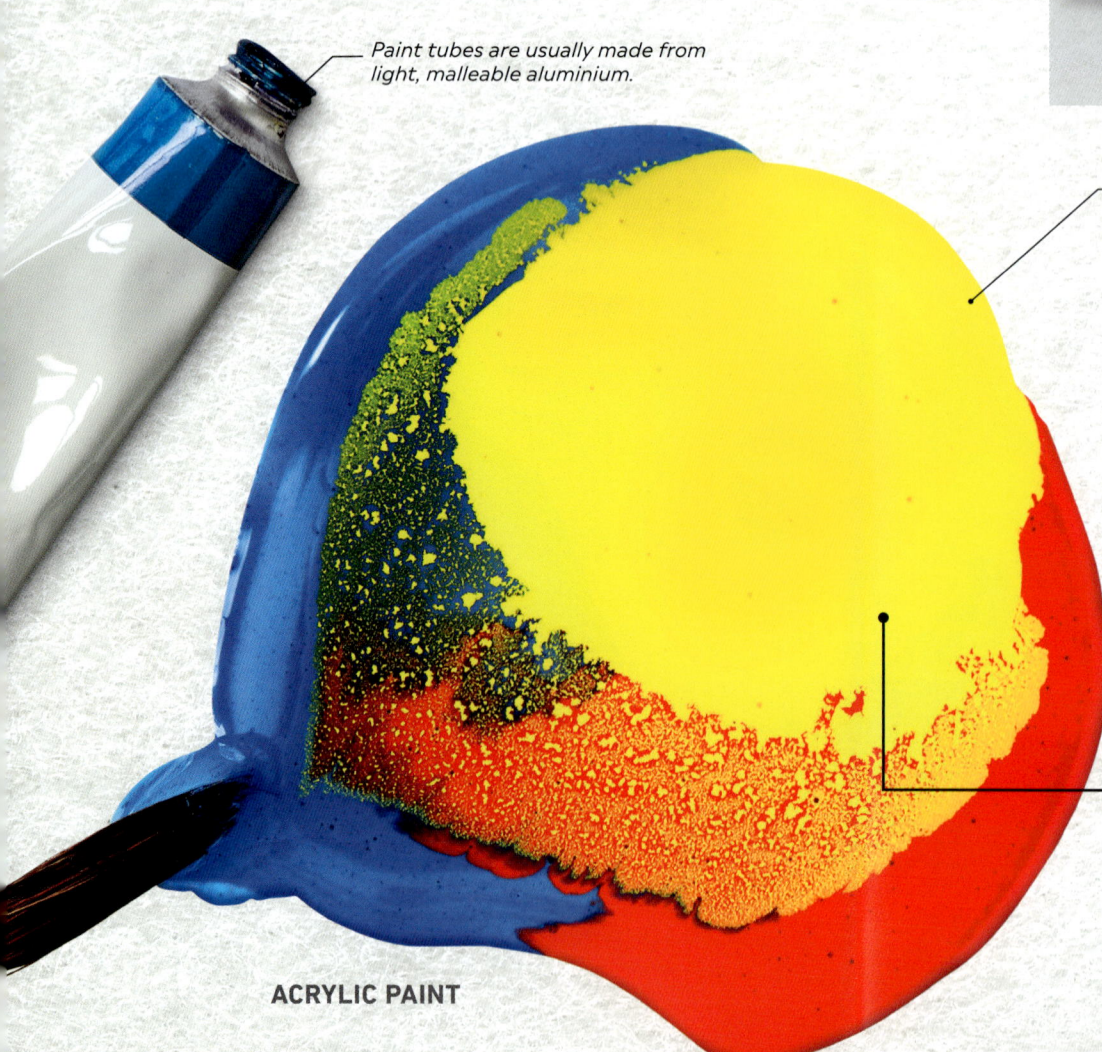

Paint tubes are usually made from light, malleable aluminium.

Acrylic paints have water added to thin them.

ACRYLIC PAINT

ACRYLIC POLYMER
Synthetic binder

This plastic material is made from acrylic acid. It is combined with water and pigments to make acrylic paint. Acrylic polymer binds the pigment in paint, and helps it form a thin film over a surface that stays in place after the water evaporates.

Carbon nanotubes stay "sticky" even when peeled off, making the gecko tape reusable.

GECKO TAPE

This adhesive tape is designed to mimic the ability of gecko lizards to cling to almost any surface with their "sticky" feet. Also called "nano tape", this tape is made up of millions of carbon nanotubes (nanoscopic hollow tubes of carbon atoms) that sit on a base of polymer tape. The weak sticky forces from each tube is multiplied by their great number so that they can grip onto surfaces.

HOW IS IT MADE?

Carbon nanotubes are made by passing a carbon-rich gas, such as methane, through a furnace at 500–1200°C (930–2200°F). The heat breaks the gas down into carbon and hydrogen. The carbon atoms react with a metal catalyst, placed on the surface of a flexible polymer, creating hollow nanotubes.

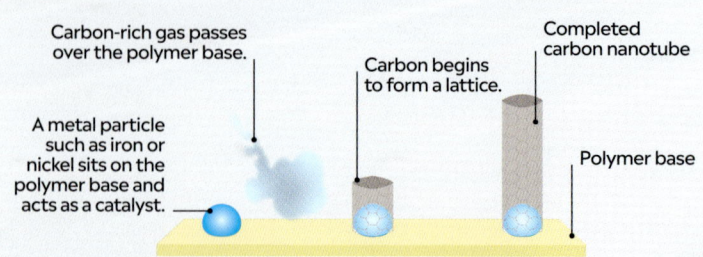

- Carbon-rich gas passes over the polymer base.
- A metal particle such as iron or nickel sits on the polymer base and acts as a catalyst.
- Carbon begins to form a lattice.
- Completed carbon nanotube
- Polymer base

The nanotubes on gecko tape are tightly packed together.

CARBON NANOTUBES
Everyday nanotechnology

This image shows the "pillars" of carbon nanotubes on the surface of a piece of gecko tape magnified about 100 times. The thin and lightweight nanotubes have a tube-like molecular structure of tightly packed carbon atoms (right) that keeps them from breaking easily and helps them withstand extreme temperatures.

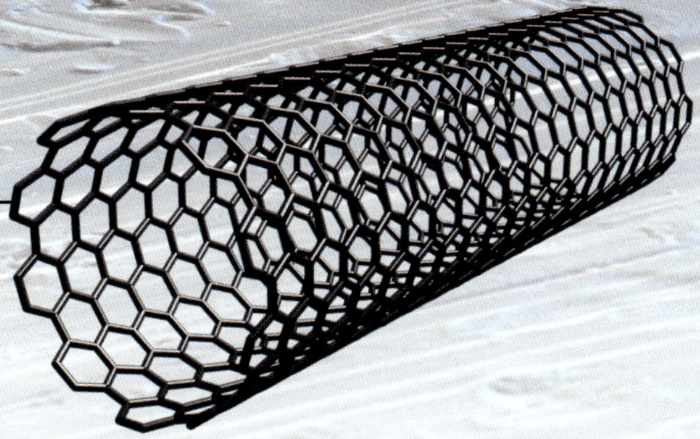

HOW DOES IT WORK?

Gecko tape mimics the "stickiness" of gecko feet, which are lined with millions of tiny hairs, called setae. These hairs give the feet a large surface area, helping the gecko stick to an object easily. The millions of carbon nanotubes in gecko tape serve the same purpose. The glue in the tape also makes it stickier.

Gecko tape

A tape made from a flexible polymer called PET is used as the base for the nanotubes.

Gecko foot clinging to glass

ELECTRIC GUITAR

An electric guitar uses pickups – copper wires coiled around magnets – to convert the vibrations of the guitar strings into electronic signals. These signals are then sent to an amplifier, which converts the signals to sounds. The materials used in the guitar affect the sounds it creates.

MAHOGANY
Warm-sounding wood

All woods have different abilities to transmit vibrations. A dense wood such as mahogany produces warm, punchy sounds that ring out for longer. By adding a layer of even denser wood like maple (as seen right), the tone becomes clearer.

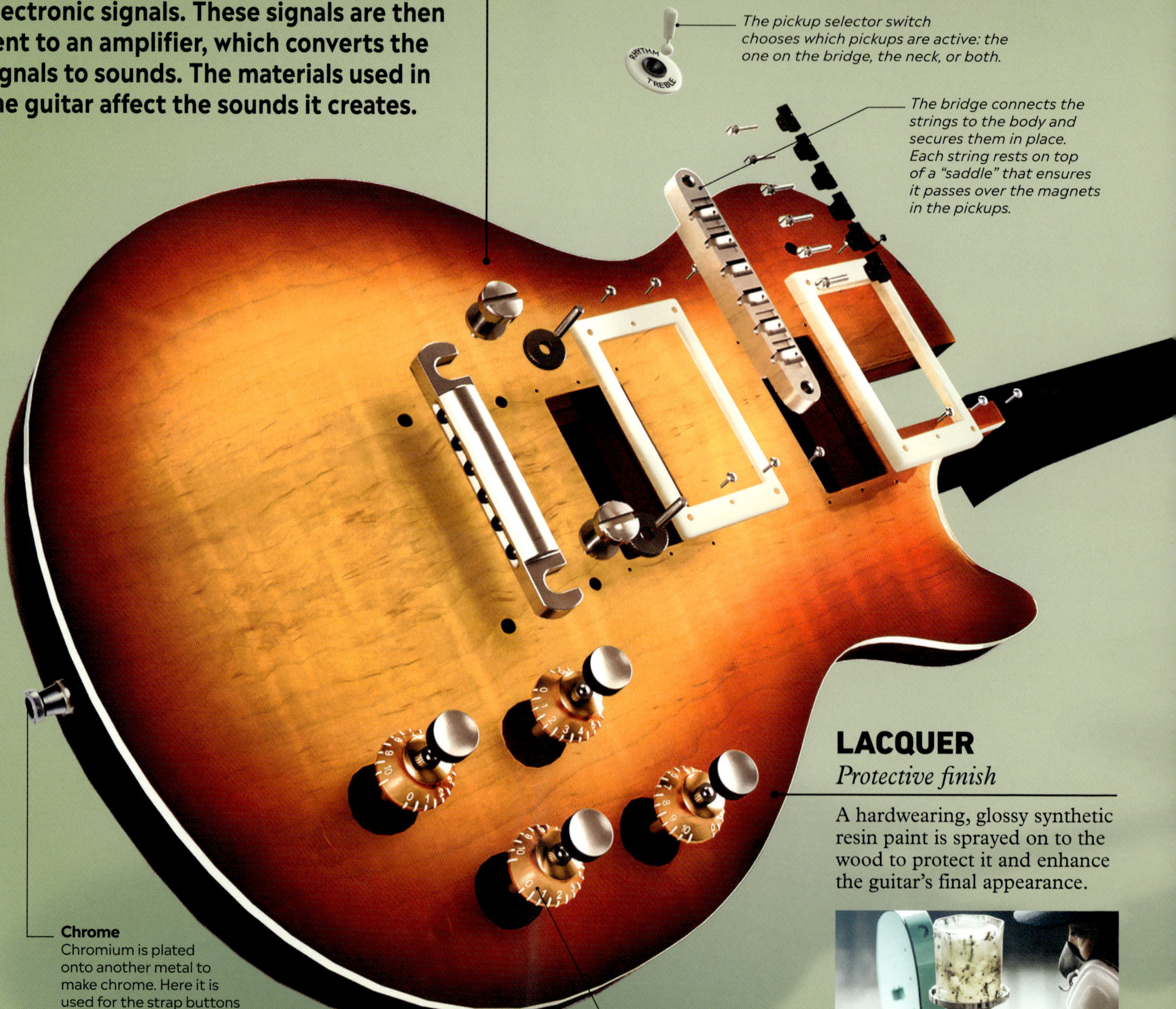

The pickup selector switch chooses which pickups are active: the one on the bridge, the neck, or both.

The bridge connects the strings to the body and secures them in place. Each string rests on top of a "saddle" that ensures it passes over the magnets in the pickups.

LACQUER
Protective finish

A hardwearing, glossy synthetic resin paint is sprayed on to the wood to protect it and enhance the guitar's final appearance.

Chrome
Chromium is plated onto another metal to make chrome. Here it is used for the strap buttons and control knobs, as it is durable, rust-resistant, and easy to clean and polish.

Control knobs for adjusting volume and tone

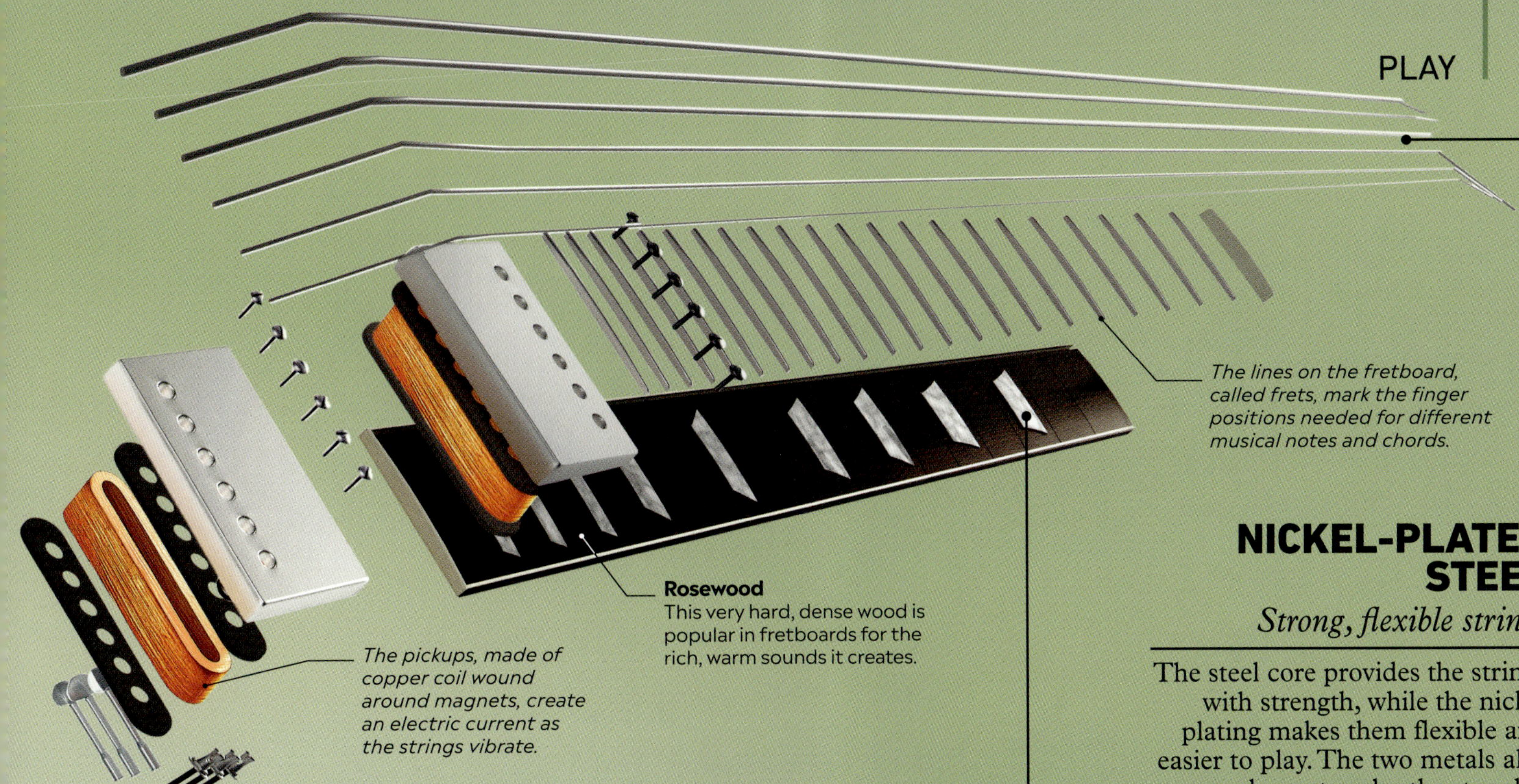

PLAY | 59

Rosewood
This very hard, dense wood is popular in fretboards for the rich, warm sounds it creates.

The lines on the fretboard, called frets, mark the finger positions needed for different musical notes and chords.

The pickups, made of copper coil wound around magnets, create an electric current as the strings vibrate.

Ebony
Used for the head, ebony works well tonally with other woods in the instrument.

NICKEL-PLATED STEEL
Strong, flexible strings

The steel core provides the strings with strength, while the nickel plating makes them flexible and easier to play. The two metals also complement each other tonally: steel creates a sharper sound, while nickel produces richer, warmer tones.

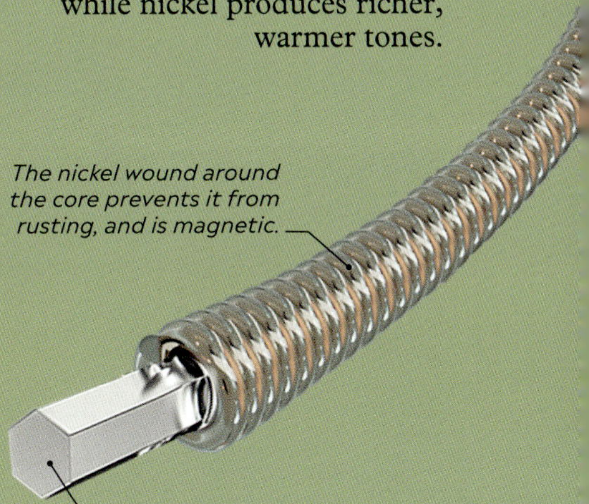

The nickel wound around the core prevents it from rusting, and is magnetic.

MOTHER-OF-PEARL
Shiny shell

This organic semi-precious material, found inside the shells of oysters and other molluscs, adds shine to the guitar neck's decorative inlays.

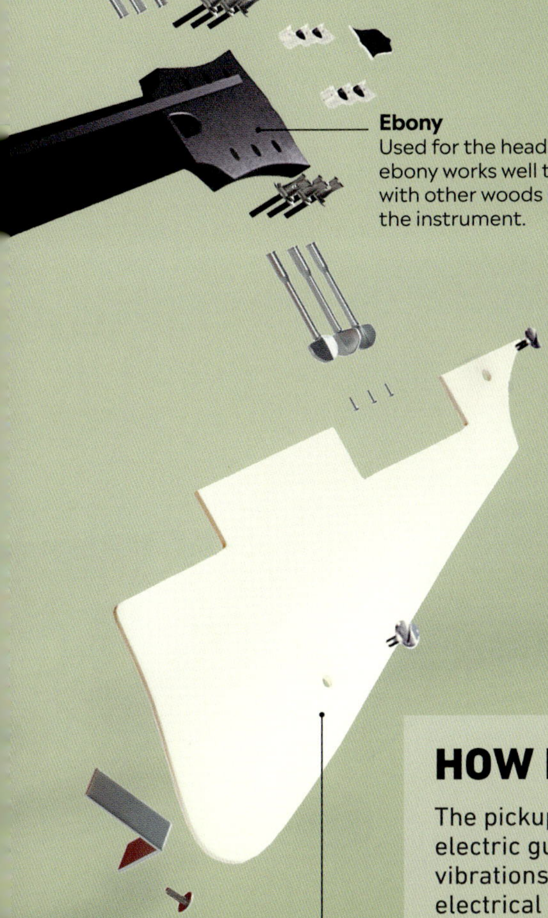

Steel
The magnetic core can withstand being tightened, stretched, and constantly vibrated.

Thermoplastic
This type of plastic can be easily moulded when hot to produce the complex shape needed for the pickguard.

HOW DOES IT WORK?

The pickups are the heart of an electric guitar. They convert the vibrations of the strings into electrical signals using coils of wire wound around magnets. The electrical signals then travel to an amplifier, which boosts them in strength and turns them into sound waves you can hear.

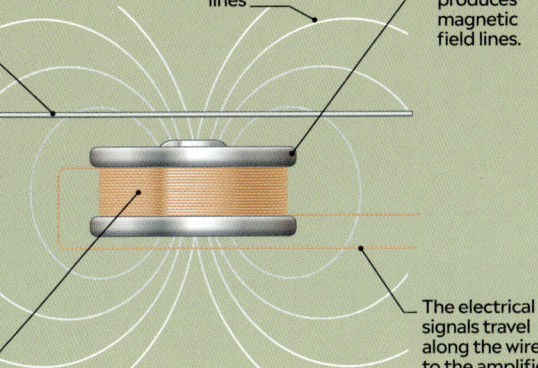

Vibrating string moves within the magnetic field.

Magnetic field lines

Magnet produces magnetic field lines.

Because the string is magnetic, its vibrations alter the magnetic field, creating weak electrical signals inside the copper coil.

The electrical signals travel along the wire to the amplifier.

PLAY

Cardboard contains many layers of thick paper, which makes it strong for heavy loads.

CARDBOARD

PAPER

PULPED WOOD

Every year, more than 200 million tonnes of wood is processed to produce pulped wood. Its uses are varied – from fluff pulp used to fill absorbent nappies to paper products.

Some towels are made with rayon, a synthetic plastic made from the cellulose in wood.

RAYON GOODS

Balsa, a light and soft hardwood, is used to make toy models.

MODEL MAKING

HARDWOOD

Strong, heavy wood from slow-growing trees that shed their leaves each year, such as oak, maple, and walnut, is known as hardwood. Most hardwoods are darker, denser, and more durable than softwoods.

Thin strips of hardwood are used to cover cheaper wood to give it a finished look.

WOOD VENEERS

FLOORING

UTENSILS

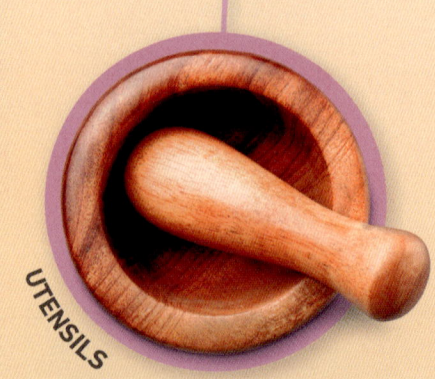

LUXURY FURNITURE

Wood can be softened with steam and then bent into intricate patterns.

WOOD IS BOTH BIODEGRADABLE AND RECYCLABLE.

USING WOOD

An important natural resource, wood has been a building material for thousands of years. Flexible, strong, and durable, it can also be carved or polished to make decorative objects. Wood is widely used for construction because it is readily available, and much lighter and easier to work with than concrete.

PLYWOOD PAVILION
Sheets of plywood are stitched together to create circular patterns.

ENGINEERED WOOD PRODUCTS
Almost every part of a tree is used. Wood chips and fibres are processed to create fibreboards and plywood, which are used in flooring, furniture, insulation, and boat building. Flexible beech plywood was used to construct a decorative arch (left) at the University of Stuttgart, Germany.

PRESSURE-TREATED TIMBER
Pressure treatment pushes fungicides and insecticides deep into the wood to protect it from termites.

MASS-PRODUCED FURNITURE

SOLID WOOD
Natural building material
Mature trees are chopped down and cut into shapes, such as planks, boards, strips, or rounded bars, at saw mills. Each tree species produces wood with its own unique colour, grain, and hardness.

SOFTWOOD
Wood from conifer trees, such as pine, cedar, and spruce, is called softwood. This wood tends to be cheaper, more flexible, and easier to work with than hardwoods.

FENCE PANELS

TIMBER FRAMES
Douglas fir, cedar, and other softwoods produce strong and sturdy house frames.

62 | PLAY

Copper
Copper wound around the bass strings makes them heavier, creating a lower pitch.

Steel
Piano strings must be very strong to resist snapping.

Hornbeam wood
Lighter and with greater elasticity than other hard woods, hornbeam hammers rebound faster.

FELT
Hitting the right tone

The hammers that hit the piano strings when a key is pressed are cloaked in wool felt, a cloth made by tangling wool fibres together. Felt is used because it produces a deep, rich tone.

Artificial ivory
Historically, white piano keys were made from ivory. Today, synthetic materials that closely mimic ivory's appearance and other properties are used.

Veneer
A thin layer of expensive-looking wood (a veneer) placed over a cheaper base wood provides an attractive appearance at a lower cost.

The strings pass over a strip of wood called the bridge, which transfers their vibrations to the soundboard.

Iron is cast into a shape by pouring the molten metal into a mould.

CAST IRON
A strong, stable metal

The plate is the one part of the piano that must not move. It is a large metal frame, sometimes called a "harp", to which the strings are attached at each end. Cast iron is typically used for the plate because it is strong and does not warp under the pressure of the strings once they are tightened.

Brass
A highly durable material with an attractive gold shine, brass is often used for piano pedals.

PLAY | 63

Acrylic
Glossy, easy-to-clean acrylic plastic is an ideal outer material for some parts of cheaper pianos.

HOW DOES IT WORK?

When a key is pressed, a felt-wrapped hammer strikes a string. This causes the string to vibrate at a specific frequency, producing a musical note. The sound of the vibrating string is transferred through the bridge to the soundboard, which amplifies the sound. Long, thick strings produce low-pitched notes and fine, short strings produce high-pitched notes.

Pressing the key
As the key is pressed, the damper moves away from the string, which is now free to vibrate. At the same time, the hammer is pushed forward to hit the string.

Releasing the key
With no pressure on the key the hammer returns to its original position and the damper moves forward to hit the string, stopping its vibration and silencing it.

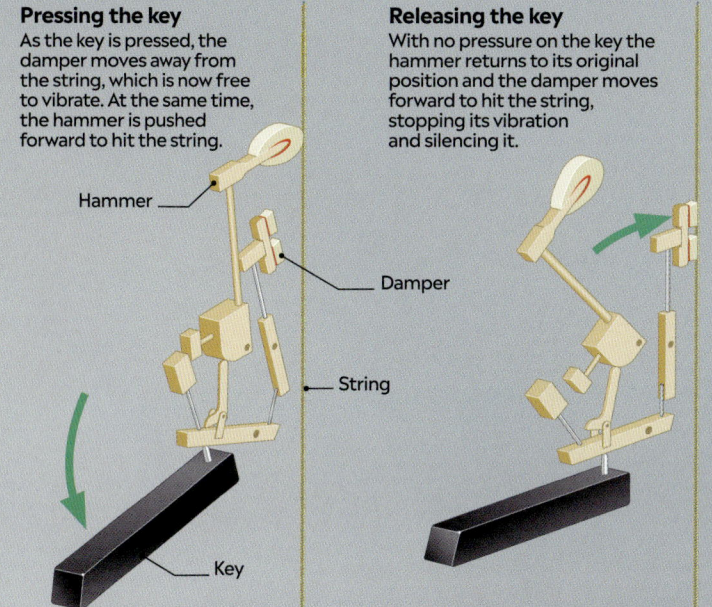

Hammer — Damper — String — Key

SPRUCE
A natural amplifier

The job of the soundboard in any stringed instrument is to amplify the sound coming from the strings. Spruce is usually the wood of choice due to its light weight and long, straight grain, which resonates and enhances any sounds that it receives.

Small wheels called castors make it easier to move the piano.

UPRIGHT PIANO

Pressing a piano's keys causes small hammers inside to strike taut steel strings. These are tuned to vibrate at different frequencies, creating musical tones. The strings and frame are horizontal in a grand piano, but vertical in an upright piano, like this one.

DRUM KIT
Modern drum kits are made from hard-wearing materials that can withstand a constant beating. Durable polyester is used for the surface of the drums as it does not shrink or expand from heat or moisture, and is long-lasting. Metal cymbals produce loud reverberating sounds when struck, and are usually made of sonorous copper alloys such as brass, which is a mixture of copper and zinc, and sometimes other metals.

PLAY

USING FABRICS

For thousands of years, fabrics have been produced for clothing, carpets, curtains, sheets, ship sails, and more. Until the invention of synthetic fibres in the 20th century, all fabrics were derived from natural sources.

Stout, strong canvas is resistant to wind and water.

CANVAS TENT

CORDUROY TROUSERS

VELVET CURTAINS

DENIM JACKET

Linen, made from fibres of the flax plant's stem, can absorb sweat.

LINEN SHIRT

SEAGRASS BASKET

COTTON
The fluffy fibres from cotton bolls (seed capsules) are processed to make various soft and breathable cotton fabrics.

Strong, robust fibres from jute plants are used to make bags.

JUTE BAG

Cotton yarn on an industrial spinning machine

PLANT-BASED FABRICS
Cloth from plant fibres

Fibres derived from plant stems, leaves, or seed capsules can be spun into yarn. Cotton is the most commonly used plant fibre in manufacturing yarn for fabrics, and is grown in more than 70 countries.

US DOLLAR BANKNOTES ARE 25% LINEN AND 75% COTTON.

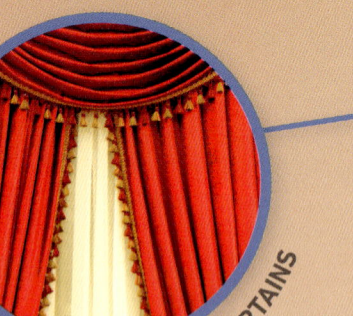

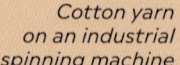
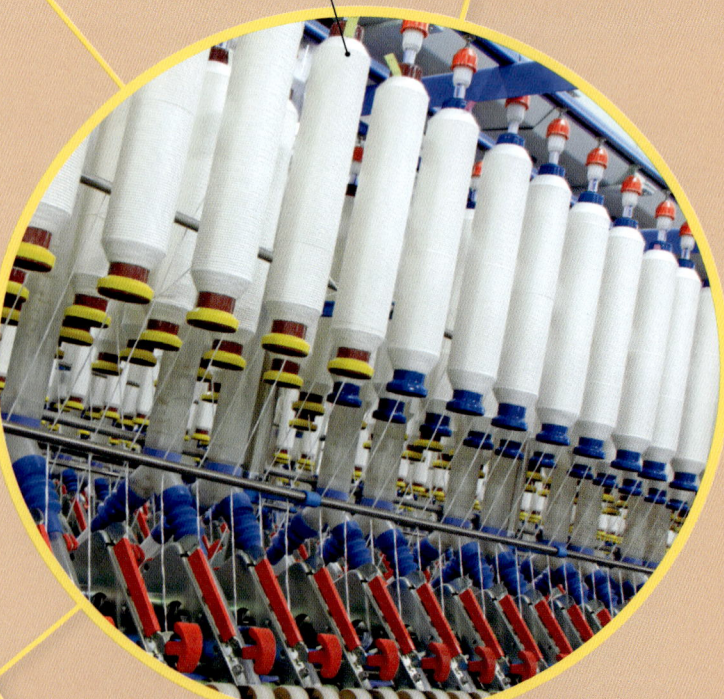

PLAY | 67

Silk yarn is obtained from cocoons spun by silkworms.

Turkish carpets, woven from wool and silk, are warm and resist dirt.

WOOL AND SILK CARPETS

SILK TIES

Leather is soft and flexible.

LEATHER BELTS

Silk is a light and durable material with a natural sheen.

ANIMAL-DERIVED FABRICS
Skins and fibres from animals

The skins and hides of some animals are processed as leather, while sheep, goat, and llama fleeces are sheared to make wool. These fabrics tend to be warm because they trap heat.

Synthetic fabric on an industrial loom

Spandex is a stretchy material used to make skin-tight clothing.

SPANDEX SPORTSWEAR

Coated nylon is light, sturdy, and airtight.

NYLON BALLOON

ACRYLIC RUG

SYNTHETIC FABRICS
Chemically produced cloth

Most synthetic fabrics are made from polymers derived from fossil fuels such as petroleum. These fabrics are usually inexpensive and can have special properties, such as water resistance.

DIAMONDS ARE SOLD IN CARATS. ONE CARAT IS 0.2 G (0.007 OZ).

JEWELLERY

A cut diamond jewel shines by refracting (bending) and reflecting light.

CUT DIAMONDS
Some diamonds are shaped and polished to form gemstones, which reflect light brilliantly. They are graded and valued based on their weight (in carats), cut, colour, and clarity.

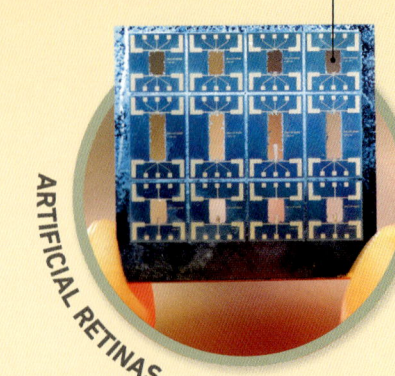

Artificial retinas contain a thin film made of diamond.

ARTIFICIAL RETINAS

Diamonds are used in watch gears, bearings, and body parts, as well as decoration, as the material doesn't wear.

DIAMOND CHIPS

RAW DIAMONDS
Ancient crystals

Most diamonds were formed 1-3 billion years ago just below Earth's crust. The intense pressure and high temperature bonded carbon atoms into hard crystals. Today, some diamonds are manufactured by mimicking these conditions, or by growing them in a chamber of carbon-rich gases.

USING DIAMONDS

A form of carbon with its atoms locked in a rigid 3D pattern, diamond is the hardest natural mineral on Earth. Diamonds dazzle, can resist many chemicals, conduct heat very well, and don't cause much friction when rubbed against another object.

ONLY 20% OF DIAMONDS ARE USED AS GEMS.

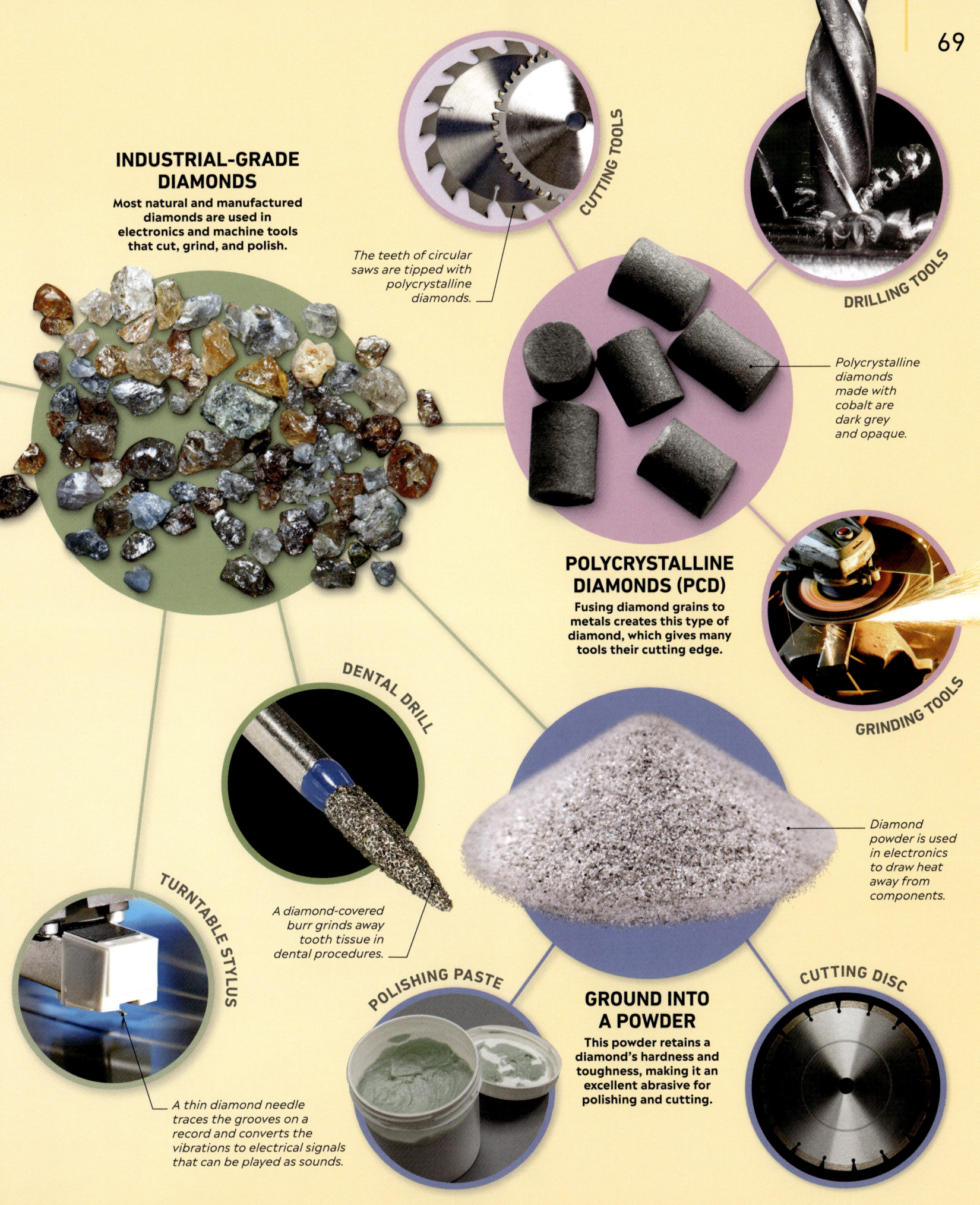

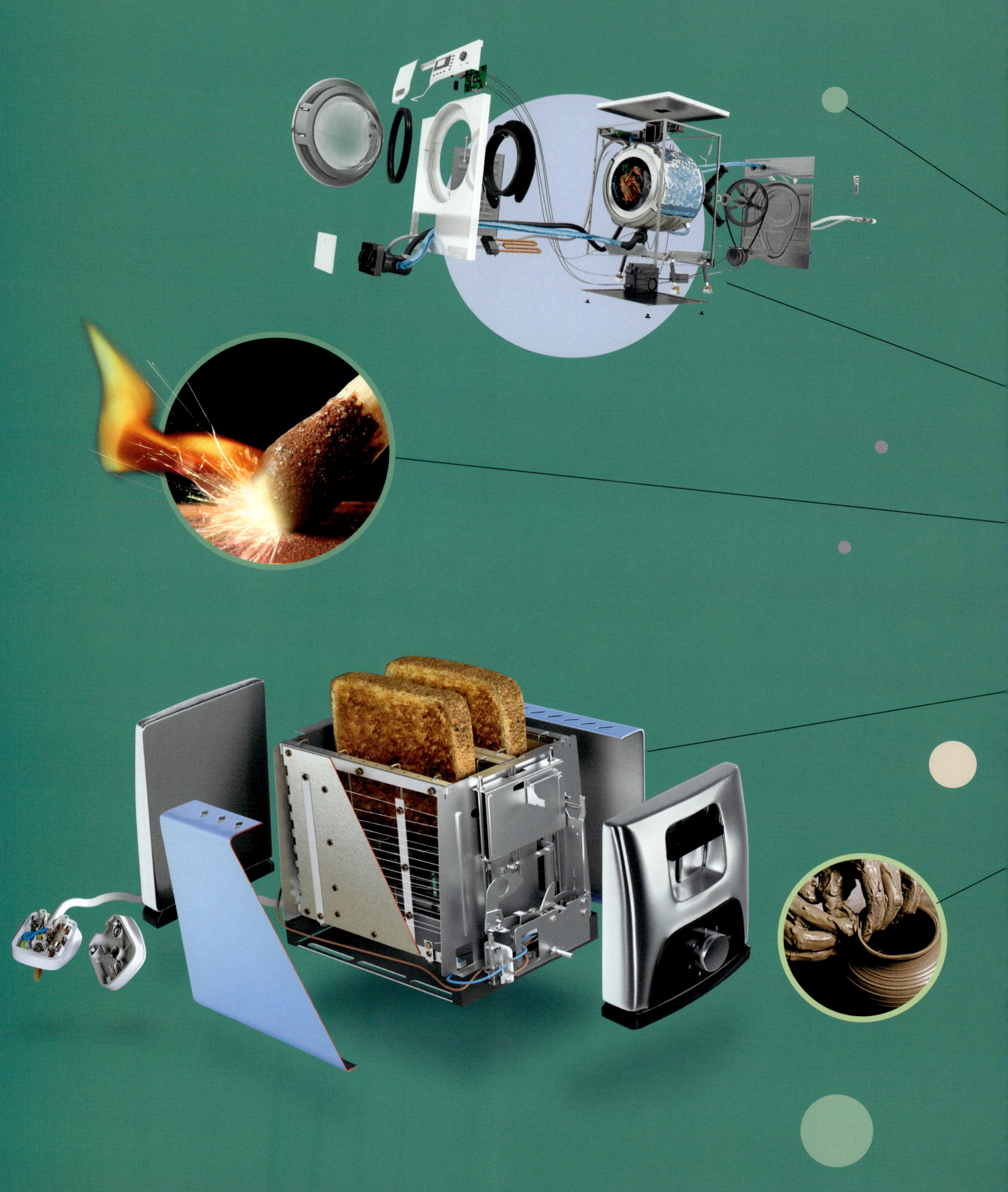

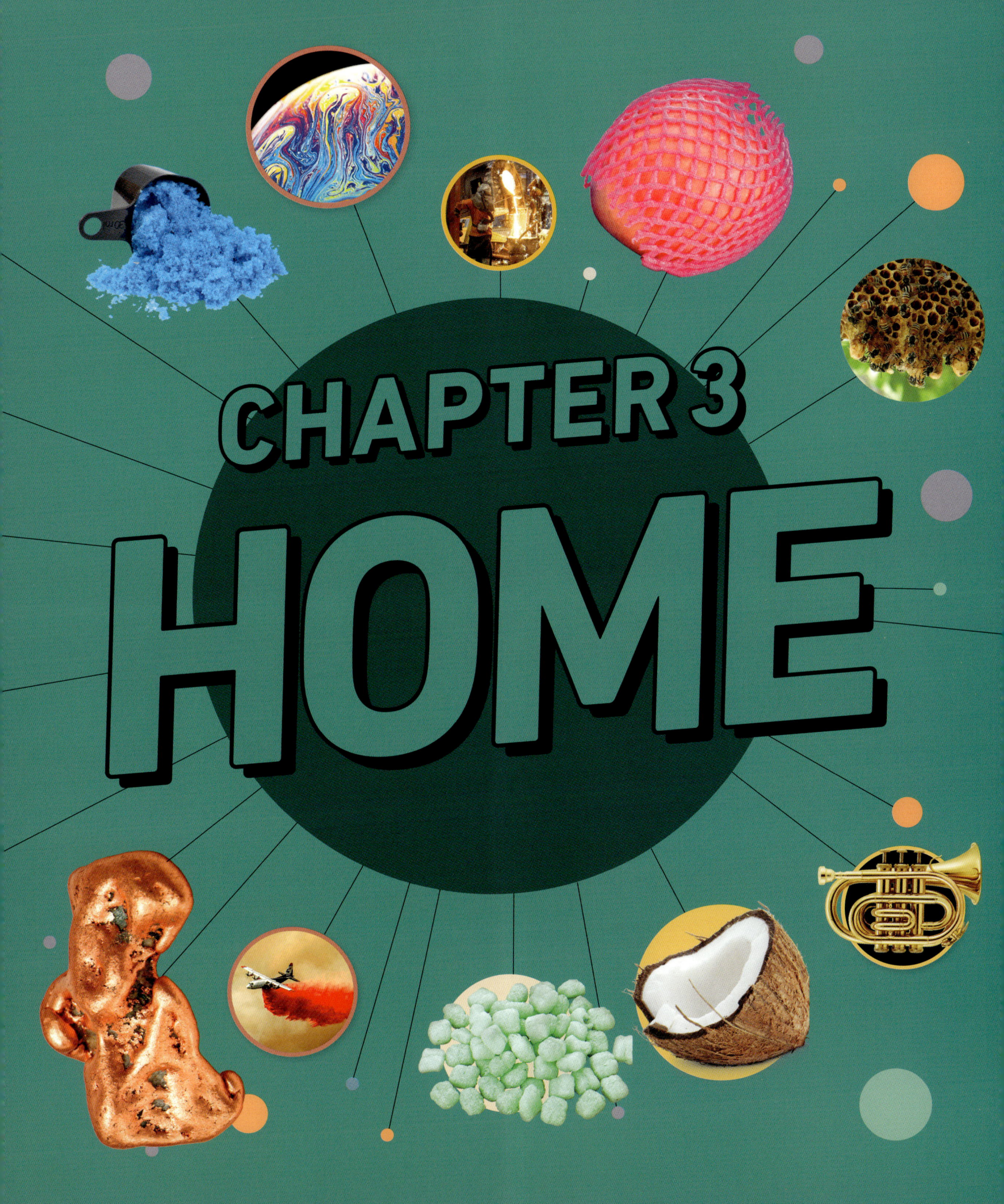

Wood
A very thin strip of wood burns easily and steadily. When it is heated, it produces gases that burn in the presence of oxygen.

HIDE GLUE
Holds it all together

Hide glue is created from collagen, a protein found in all animals. It is made by boiling connective tissue, such as bones and tendons, from carcasses. The glue binds all the other materials together on the head of the match.

GLASS POWDER
Scratchy surface

Glass is milled into small particles to make glass powder. Coarse glass powder is coated on the match head and strike pad to increase the friction between them. This friction is necessary to generate enough heat to ignite the match.

Potassium chlorate
This chemical in the match head breaks down and releases oxygen when burnt.

Coating the stick in paraffin wax protects it from moisture and helps the flame continue to burn evenly as it travels down the match.

STRIKING A MATCH

Modern matches are made from tiny wooden splints with a coated end. The coating is made of flammable materials such as potassium chlorate and sulphur, which ignite from the heat produced by striking the match against a strike pad containing red phosphorus.

ANTIMONY TRISULPHIDE
Burns in air

The match head contains flammable antimony trisulphide as a fuel. This material keeps the match from going out too quickly. Antimony trisulphide is processed from the mineral stibnite (left).

RED PHOSPHORUS
Transforms and ignites

This chemical is used on the strike pad of matchboxes. Striking the pad with the match head creates friction. The heat produced by the friction turns the red phosphorus into white phosphorus, which ignites spontaneously in the air.

HOW IS IT MADE?

To make matches, wood is first sliced into thin sheets, which are then cut into tiny splints. These splints are dipped in a chemical bath, dried, and then dipped in melted paraffin. Once the paraffin has dried, the striking end of the splint is coated with liquid chemicals to form the "match head". The matches are then dried out for a final time before being packaged.

Matches are dipped into the solution in batches for about five seconds.

Creating the match head

FIRE RETARDANT

To keep forest fires from getting out of control, firefighting planes spray a substance that suppresses the flames and coats the unburnt vegetation to prevent it from catching fire. This fire retardant contains water and chemicals, such as ammonium phosphate and ammonium sulphate. The retardant gets its red colour from iron oxide, which helps pilots know how much ground they have covered.

ELECTRIC TOASTER

Many of us take the humble toaster for granted, but this small kitchen appliance makes clever use of different materials. For instance, the toaster's auto pop-up function combines two metals that respond differently to heat, giving users precise control over how much their bread is toasted.

THE "POP-UP" TOASTER WAS INVENTED IN 1919.

Pop-up spring pushes the bread up out of its slot once toasted.

Pressing the lever down to lower the bread into its slot compresses a spring beneath.

Steel
Steel is a popular material for toaster frames, as it can withstand high temperatures without warping.

HOW DOES IT WORK?

The timer in a toaster uses a bimetallic strip – two different metals sandwiched together – to switch off when the strip reaches a certain temperature. As they are heated, one metal expands more than the other, causing the strip to bend until the electrical contact breaks, opening the circuit and stopping the current.

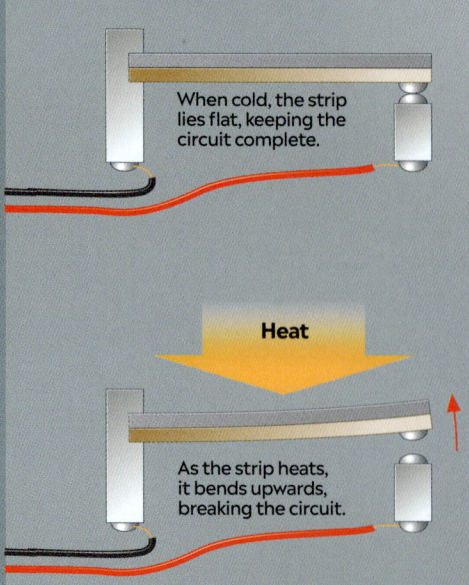

When cold, the strip lies flat, keeping the circuit complete.

Heat

As the strip heats, it bends upwards, breaking the circuit.

Polypropylene
This plastic is easily coloured and can be moulded into any shape, making it suitable for the toaster's outer casing.

Copper
Electrical cable contains wire made of copper, a good conductor of electricity.

The timer button controls how long the bread is toasted by adjusting how far the bimetallic strip needs to bend to break the circuit.

NICHROME WIRE
Red hot filament

The glowing red wires inside the toaster are made from nichrome, an alloy of nickel and chromium. Nichrome is often used to heat things due to its high electrical resistance, which means it radiates a lot of heat when a current runs through it.

Mica crystals naturally occur in a flat, sheet-like form.

MICA
Heat-resistant mineral

Mica is a mineral that can be easily split into large, flat "sheets". The heating wires inside the toaster are woven around a sheet of mica, as the material is resistant to heat and a good electrical insulator.

PVC
Flexible PVC insulates the copper wire to prevent users getting electric shocks.

Powder coating
The toaster's exterior panels are sprayed with a toughening powder made of resins before being cured in an oven. This process creates a thick finish that is more durable than conventional paint.

STEATITE
Electrical insulator

Steatite, also known as soapstone, is a very soft type of rock that is popular in electrical devices, including plug fuses, because of its insulating properties. This means a sudden electrical power surge will not overload the appliance.

78 | HOME

MICROWAVE OVEN

This kitchen device can cook food faster than a conventional oven by using microwaves – a form of electromagnetic radiation, like visible light and radio waves. These microwaves are sent into and trapped inside a sealed steel cooking chamber. The radiation makes the water molecules inside the food vibrate, and this action heats up the food.

THE FIRST COMMERCIAL MICROWAVE OVEN STOOD 1.7 M (5.5 FT) TALL.

An LED display shows time and power settings.

The control panel electronics send signals to start and stop the magnetron.

Artificial rubber
Flexible, moisture-proof rubber helps form a tight seal around the microwave's window.

STEEL
Microwave reflector

Embedded in the door glass is a thin steel sheet that reflects microwaves back into the cooking chamber. The sheet contains hundreds of small holes so the user can see into the chamber. These holes are smaller than the wavelength of a microwave, so microwaves cannot escape.

The door button is loaded with a spring that, when pushed, releases the latch to let the oven door open.

HOW DOES IT WORK?

The magnetron emits microwaves that pass along a waveguide into the cooking chamber. When the microwaves enter the food, they excite its water molecules, causing them to vibrate and generate heat through the friction of the molecules jostling and rubbing together. A turntable rotates the food to help it cook evenly.

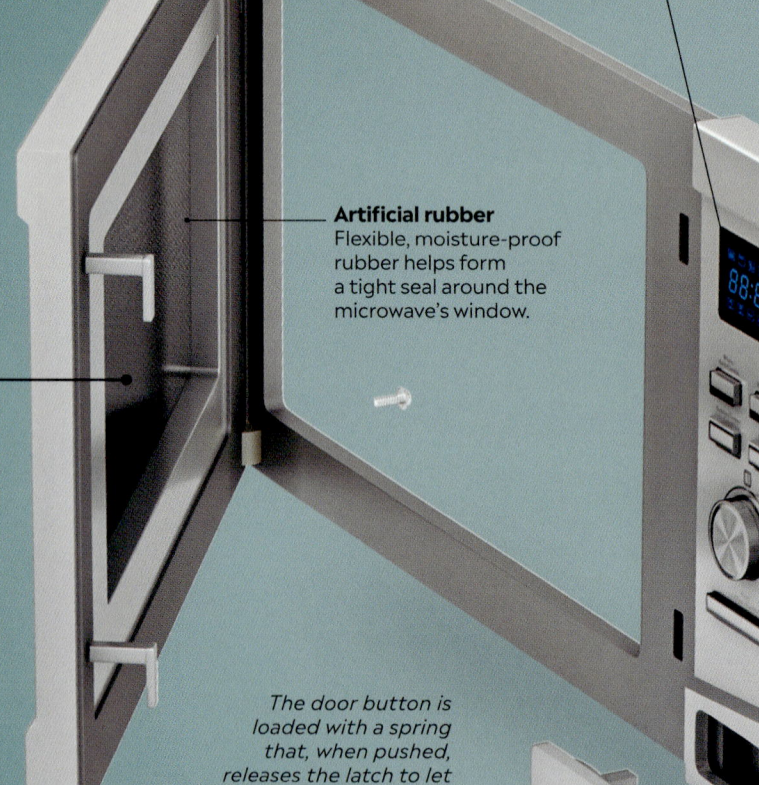

Wave stirrer scatters microwaves.

Microwaves reflect off steel walls towards food.

Waveguide directs microwaves towards cooking chamber.

Magnetron generates microwaves.

Dial allows user to select cooking time and power level.

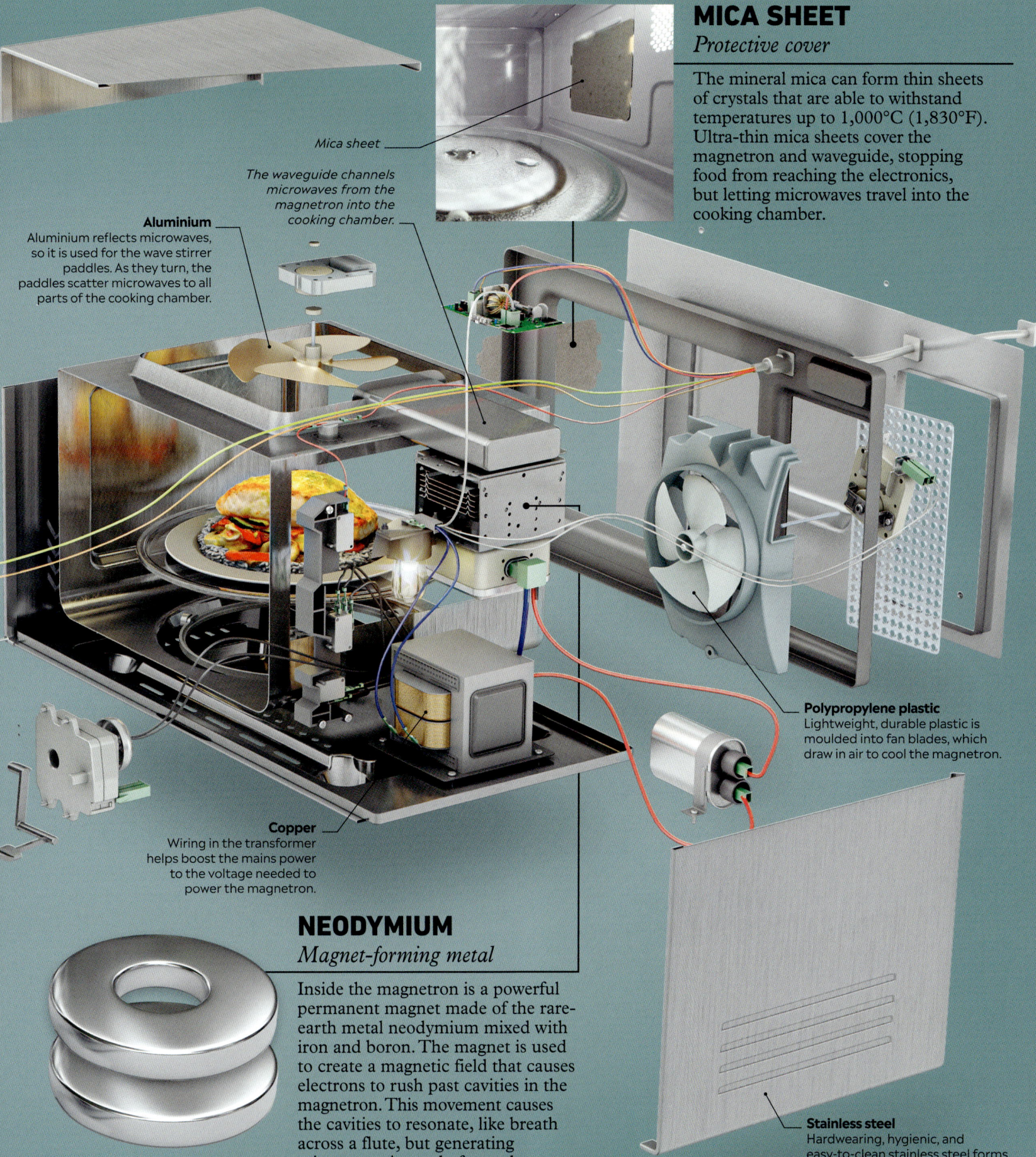

BEESWAX
Eco-friendly wax

Honeybees produce a natural wax that they use to construct their honeycombs. When warmed, beeswax becomes soft and flexible. It can be used to coat cotton fabrics and to make waterproof and food-safe reusable wrappers.

BEESWAX WRAPPER

SUGAR CANE TRAY

HOW IS BUBBLE WRAP MADE?

Bubble wrap is made by passing two layers of polyethylene film between two rollers. The top roller has several tiny holes. A vacuum applies suction through these holes creating tiny pockets or bubbles in the top sheet. At the same time, the rollers squeeze the top and bottom sheets together, sealing in the air pockets, which form little bubbles.

Low-density polyethylene (LDPE)
This flexible and moisture-resistant plastic is found in various types of packaging including cling film and bubble wrap.

BUBBLE WRAP

Roller with holes
Top sheet
Films pulled through rollers
Bottom sheet
Rolling process

Air trapped in the bubbles
Finished bubble wrap

BAGASSE FIBRE
Non-toxic and compostable

When juice is extracted from sugar cane it leaves behind a material called bagasse fibre. This can absorb excess moisture, resist grease, and withstand high temperatures making it suitable for creating food containers.

Aluminium
Thin, pliable aluminium sheets, sometimes coated with plastic, are used to make airtight bags that protect their contents from moisture.

ALUMINIUM FOIL BAG

PACKAGING

From bubble wrap to aluminium foil, different forms of packaging are essential to hold, carry, and protect a range of everyday items. The kind of material used depends on the item being packaged and how it needs to be protected. For example, fruit is wrapped in foam nets to keep it from bruising, while coffee beans are sealed in airtight bags to maintain their freshness.

Cornstarch
Packing peanuts made from cornstarch have a low impact on the environment as they decompose over time and can be added to compost heaps.

COMPOSTABLE PACKING PEANUTS

POLYSTYRENE FOAM NET

PAPER PULP
Recycled and recyclable

This fibrous material is derived from wood and recycled paper. It is cheap, durable, and used to create corrugated cardboard for shipping and storage.

Polystyrene
The polymer polystyrene is used to produce foam, an airy material with excellent shock absorption. It can act as protective packaging for delicate objects. Foam is also easy to transport as it is lightweight.

A layer of thick, wavy paper is placed between two sheets of thinner paper to make this sturdy cardboard.

CORRUGATED CARDBOARD

USING COPPER

Soft and easy to shape, copper is a metal that has been used by humans to fashion tools, jewellery, and cookware for more than 7,000 years. It is still important today because it conducts heat and electricity well, and can combine with other materials to form useful alloys and compounds.

HEAT TRANSFER

Copper is one of the best of all metals at conducting heat. It is used in making fermentation tanks and boilers, and to build the tubes for solar water heaters and refrigerators.

Copper fermentation tanks are used in breweries for even heat distribution.

A shiny lustre and an unusual colour make copper jewellery popular.

COPPER JEWELLERY

Copper pipes resist corrosion and carry hot and cold water around buildings.

PLUMBING

CIRCUIT BOARD

COPPER WIRE

Copper is extremely ductile, meaning it can be easily made into wire. One of the best conductors of electricity among metals (second only to silver) it is used on printed circuit boards and for electrical wiring.

COPPER NUGGET
Conductive metal

Copper is a common, reddish metal. Copper ore is mined from sedimentary rock. The ores are processed to remove impurities and extract the metal from the rock.

MOTOR WINDINGS

Metres of copper wire are coiled in this drill motor.

The outer surface of a US 25-cent "quarter" coin is made of cupronickel.

US 25-CENT COIN

CUPRONICKEL
This silver-coloured alloy contains 60–90% copper as well as nickel and a little iron or manganese to strengthen it. Cupronickel resists corrosion by saltwater, so it is used in water pipes and marine engineering.

SHIP PROPELLER

Propellers of some boats and ships are constructed from cupronickel.

MORE THAN 75% OF ALL THE COPPER EVER MINED IS STILL IN USE TODAY.

A trumpet's body is made from brass, an alloy of copper and zinc.

BRASS MUSICAL INSTRUMENT

COPPER COMPOUNDS
Copper is a key ingredient in many industrial chemical compounds, such as the cupric chloride used to set dyes on fabrics, and hydrated copper sulphate (below), which is used in water purifiers and pesticides.

COPPER ALLOYS
Copper is mixed with other metals, such as zinc or nickel, to form strong and durable alloys. Around 5,500 years ago, people learned to alloy copper with arsenic and tin to make strong, hard bronze, which was ideal for statues, tools, and weapons.

BRONZE STATUE

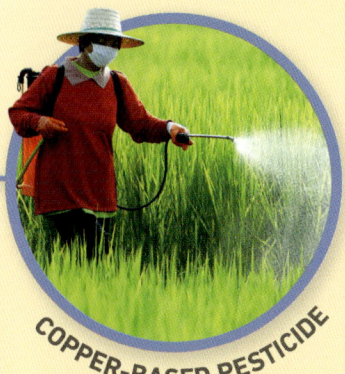

COPPER-BASED PESTICIDE

Bronze is a popular material for statues because it is easy to shape and corrodes very slowly.

WASHING MACHINE

Washing machines clean clothes by tumbling them around in plenty of soapy water. The clothes rubbing against each other and the inside of the drum loosens dirt, the soap molecules lift it away, and finally the high-speed spin cycle pushes the dirty water out through holes in the drum.

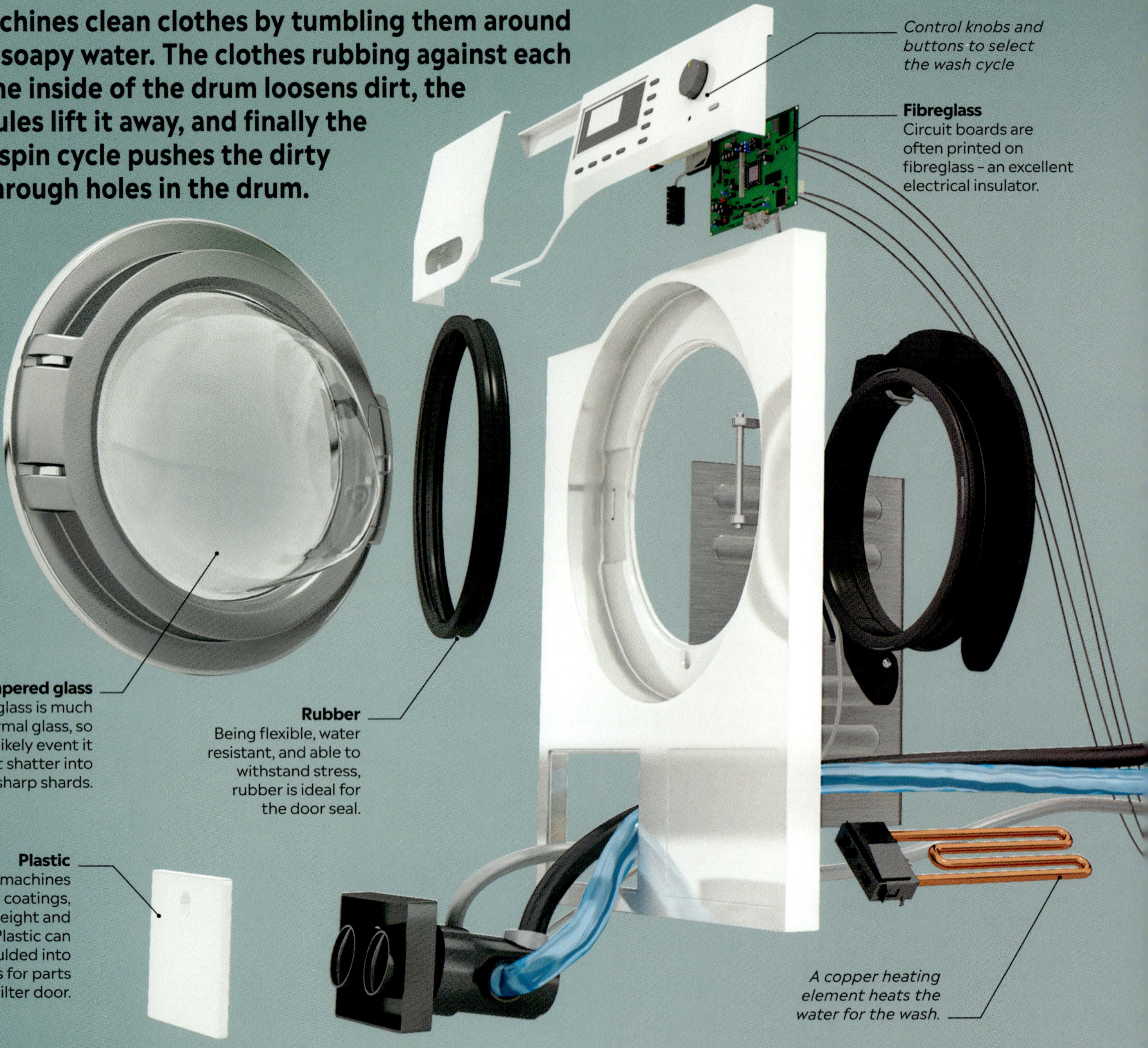

Control knobs and buttons to select the wash cycle

Fibreglass
Circuit boards are often printed on fibreglass – an excellent electrical insulator.

Tempered glass
This safety glass is much tougher than normal glass, so that – in the unlikely event it breaks – it won't shatter into small, sharp shards.

Rubber
Being flexible, water resistant, and able to withstand stress, rubber is ideal for the door seal.

Plastic
Most washing machines have plastic coatings, which are lightweight and easy to clean. Plastic can also be moulded into complex shapes for parts such as this filter door.

A copper heating element heats the water for the wash.

HOW DOES IT WORK?

A washing machine uses movement to create the friction that loosens dirt. An electric motor drives the motion of the drum. It is connected to the back of the drum via a belt-and-pulley system, which multiplies the force of the motor, allowing its thin, rotating spindle to turn the much larger drum.

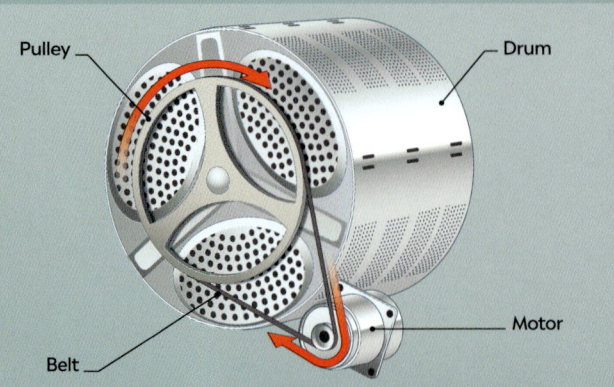

Pulley — Drum — Motor — Belt

THE EARLIEST WASHING MACHINES HAD WOODEN BARRELS.

PVC
Flexible plastic

Polyvinyl chloride (PVC) is a type of plastic widely used in plumbing. Flexible PVC is suitable for the wastewater hose, making it easy to bend and fit in the space behind the machine.

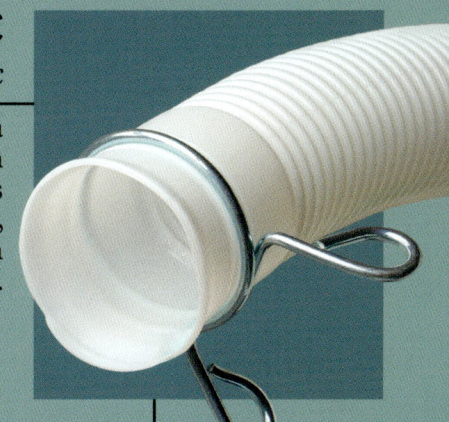

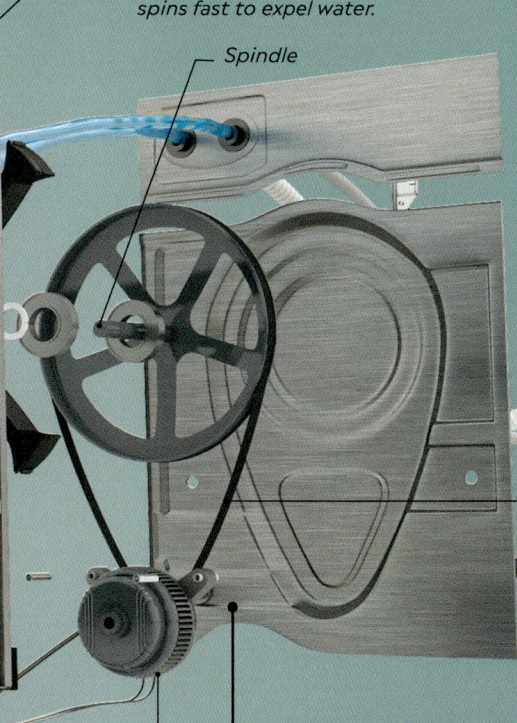

Stainless steel
Resistant to corrosion and rusting, stainless steel is perfect for this wet environment.

Springs help to absorb the drum's movements, especially when it spins fast to expel water.

Spindle

Rubber belt linking the motor to the spindle that attaches to the back of the drum

Motor

GALVANIZED STEEL
Rust-resistant metal

By coating steel with zinc (galvanizing), it becomes resistant to corrosion. The steel is submerged in molten zinc which, once solidified, is waterproof. The steel is then pressed into sheets (below) for use in washing machines, dishwashers, and marine structures.

PORCELAIN ENAMEL
Protective coating

Best known for making fine chinaware, porcelain is often used in machines for its heat- and stain-resistant qualities. Applying a thin layer of this ceramic to the metal drum also provides a smooth surface that is gentle on clothes.

SOAP BUBBLE

A soap bubble, made from dish soap and water, has a thin skin with multiple layers. When light hits these layers, some colours are absorbed and others are reflected on the surface of the bubble. Which colours are reflected depends on the thickness of the layers. Thicker patches are green and the colours change to blue, then pink, and finally yellow as the bubble thins.

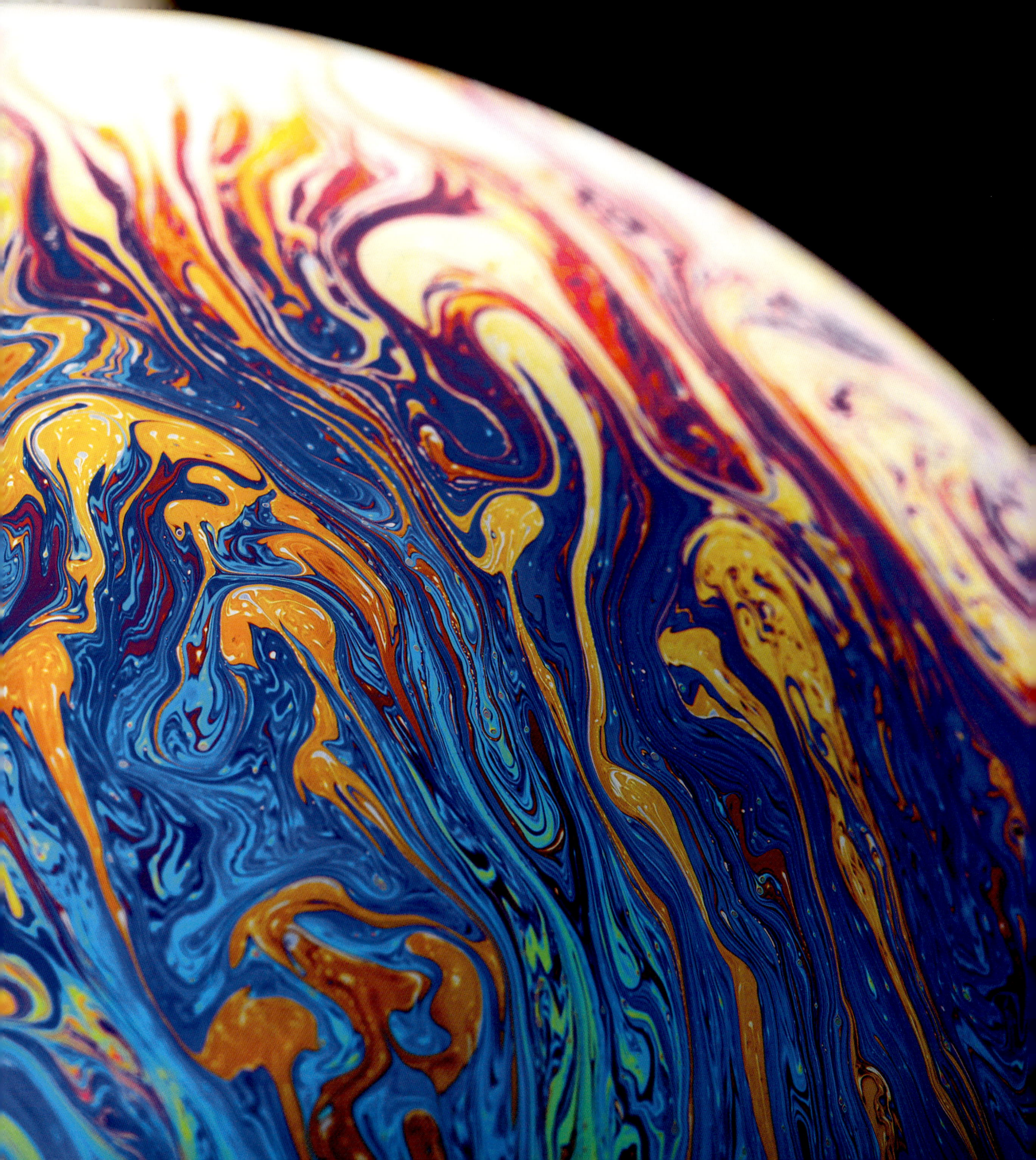

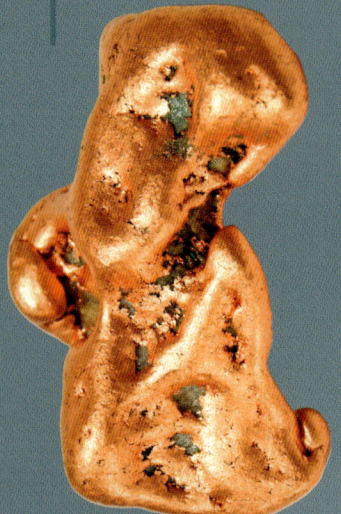

COPPER
Heat-conducting metal

Not only is copper easy to fashion into pipes, but it also conducts heat extremely well. Heat can pass easily from inside the fridge and through the walls of the copper tubing into the evaporator where it is absorbed by refrigerant (see below).

HOW DOES IT WORK?

A substance called refrigerant is the key to keeping the interior of a fridge cool. Refrigerant is pumped around the fridge through copper tubing, transforming from liquid to gas and back again as it draws in warm air from inside and releases hot air outside the fridge.

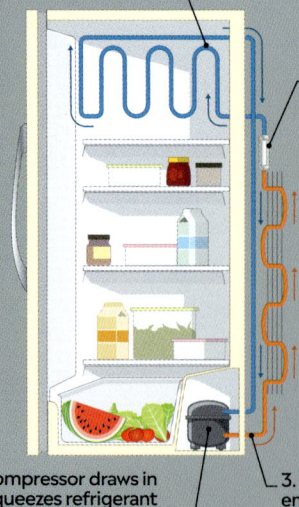

1. Refrigerant gas draws in heat from the fridge, cooling the interior.
2. Compressor draws in and squeezes refrigerant gas, increasing its pressure and temperature.
3. Hot refrigerant emits heat as it flows outside the fridge.
4. Expansion device lowers pressure of refrigerant, turning it to gas as it re-enters the fridge

Galvanized steel
Strong sheets of galvanized steel are shaped to form the frame and side panels.

Polystyrene
Rigid polystyrene called high-impact polystyrene (HIPS) is typically used to make the inner lining and moulded shapes inside a refrigerator.

FRIDGE FREEZER

These common household appliances work by transferring heat from inside the fridge freezer to the outside. By maintaining a constant low temperature within, fridge freezers slow down the growth of bacteria, keeping food fresh and increasing how long it can be safely stored.

HOME | 89

Synthetic rubber
Flexible rubber forms an airtight seal when the door is closed – vital for keeping cool air inside the fridge freezer.

Tempered glass
Glass is heat-treated or chemically-treated to strengthen and toughen it for use as shelving.

LDPE plastic
Food-safe low-density polyethylene (LDPE) plastic tubing carries water to the dispenser.

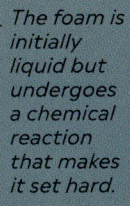

The foam is initially liquid but undergoes a chemical reaction that makes it set hard.

POLYURETHANE FOAM
Expanding plastic foam

Polyurethane foam is injected between the fridge freezer's outer case and its plastic liner. It expands in volume by more than 30 times to fill the space within the void. When set hard, the solid foam is an excellent thermal insulator, keeping all the coolness inside the fridge freezer.

Chilled, filtered water is dispensed from a water reservoir inside the fridge freezer.

ABS plastic
Acrylonitrile butadiene styrene (ABS) is a hard, impact-resistant plastic used to make the durable door handles.

COCONUT CARBON
Carbon cleaning granules

The husks (hairy outer shells) of coconuts are used for water filters. Husks are charred by heating them to 500–600°C (930–1100°F), then treated with chemicals or steam to form "activated" carbon. Microscopic pores in this carbon filter out impurities such as chlorine, while allowing clean water to pass through.

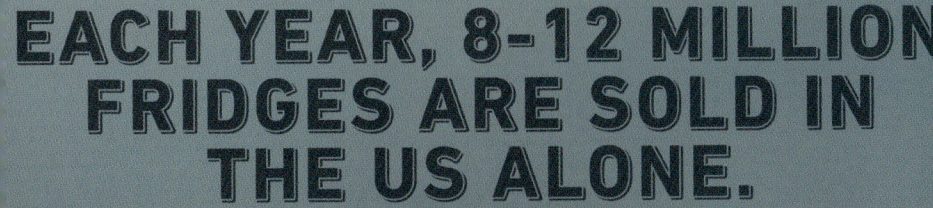

EACH YEAR, 8–12 MILLION FRIDGES ARE SOLD IN THE US ALONE.

CLAY POTTERY

Wet clay can be easily shaped by hand into pots, vases, and other forms, making it a popular material in traditional pottery. Spinning the clay on a potter's wheel ensures that it is shaped evenly, producing perfectly symmetrical objects. Once shaped and dried, these objects are fired at high temperatures until hardened into ceramic, and then glazed and painted.

USING CERAMICS

Ceramics are materials that can be made extremely hard, brittle, and non-reactive to most chemicals when heated to very high temperatures. They include everyday objects such as bricks and porcelain, as well as high-tech components for computers, cars, and even rockets.

Molten steel being poured into ceramic moulds

MOULD IN METAL INDUSTRY

KILN BRICKS

REFRACTORY MATERIALS
These ceramics have a very high melting point. They are used to line kilns and to make moulds, ladles, and other tools that handle hot metals and molten glass.

STONEWARE

Coade stone is a ceramic made of clay, glass, flint, and terracotta.

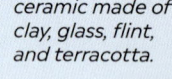

An excavator is used to dig up clay from a quarry.

POTTERY MATERIALS
Stoneware, earthenware, terracotta, and porcelain are all pottery materials made of clay. They are fired in a type of large oven called a kiln until hardened.

TRADITIONAL CERAMICS
Pliable natural materials

Traditional ceramics are made from materials that are abundant in nature, such as clays, quartz sand, and feldspar. These are among the oldest objects shaped or crafted by humans.

EARTHENWARE

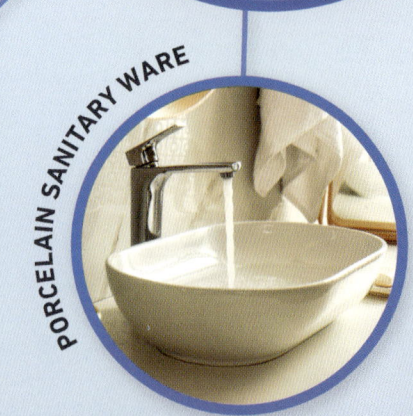

PORCELAIN SANITARY WARE

SOME CERAMICS REMAIN SOLID AT TEMPERATURES UP TO 3,800°C (6,900°F).

HOME | 93

Composite ceramic nozzles can withstand temperatures up to 3,200°C (5,800°F).

ROCKET ENGINE NOZZLES

Ceramic brake discs work well even at the high temperatures caused by frequent braking.

CERAMIC BRAKE DISCS

COMPOSITE CERAMICS
Strengthening materials, such as carbon fibre, are mixed with ceramics to create tough composites that can also tolerate very high temperatures.

Ceramics such as boron carbide provide protection in armoured vests.

ARMOUR

NON-OXIDE CERAMICS
Elements such as nitrogen and carbon are used to make extremely strong, stiff, and shock-resistant ceramics. They are used in cutting tools and car parts.

Tough silicon carbide is used in abrasives.

BEARINGS

ADVANCED CERAMICS
Manufactured synthetic materials
Chemical compounds are used to make advanced ceramics in factories. These enhanced materials are extremely hard, and resistant to stress, heat, and electricity.

A magnified image showing the surface of the composite ceramic beryllia (beryllium oxide), a material whose heat-resistance makes it useful in nuclear reactors.

Zirconium dioxide is used to make gemstones and sharp knife blades.

The ball of hip prosthetics is often made of oxide ceramics, such as alumina (aluminium oxide), which are hard-wearing.

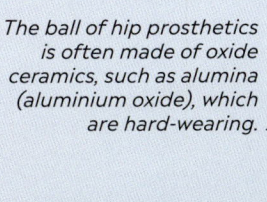

REPLACEMENT JOINTS

OXIDE CERAMICS
Oxygen is combined with materials such as aluminium, zirconium, or silicon to produce ceramics that are hard and resistant to corrosion. They are used in lasers, microchips, and other electronics.

FAUX DIAMONDS

TOOTHPASTE

We brush our teeth with a gel called toothpaste to keep them healthy. It contains many substances that perform different jobs – abrasives remove plaque, fluoride prevents tooth decay, and foaming agents called surfactants spread the toothpaste evenly in the mouth.

DIATOMACEOUS EARTH
Powdered fossils

Diatomaceous earth is a soft rock formed from the fossils of microscopic hard-shelled algae called diatoms. It can be ground down into a powder, which acts as a mild abrasive suitable for cleaning teeth.

FLUORIDE
Strengthens enamel

Sodium fluoride is a naturally occurring mineral added to most toothpastes to prevent tooth decay. It strengthens the outer covering of teeth, called enamel, protecting them from acid-forming bacteria.

PEPPERMINT
The taste of freshness

The leaves of this aromatic herb contains menthol, a chemical that produces a cooling sensation in the mouth. Peppermint is added to toothpaste to provide a "fresh" flavour.

The head cap and screw are made of hard plastic that holds its shape.

Sodium lauryl sulphate
This chemical makes the toothpaste foam.

The tube has layers of soft plastic so that it can be squeezed easily.

Between 20 and 40 per cent of toothpaste is water.

Glycerol
This colourless, sweet liquid traps water in the toothpaste to help keep the paste smooth and prevent it from drying out and crumbling in the tube.

HOW DOES IT WORK?

When you squeeze a tube of striped toothpaste, you push the main colour into a small outlet pipe. This also forces the stripe colours, held in separate pipes on either side of the main colour, into the main outlet pipe through holes. The combined paste that exits the tube through the nozzle now has a striped effect.

A BLOB OF TOOTHPASTE ON THE BRUSH IS CALLED A NURDLE.

Start of outlet pipe · Stripe colour · Hole in outlet pipe · Nozzle
Main colour
Inside of a striped toothpaste tube · Stripe colour · Hole in outlet pipe · Striped toothpaste

Nylon bristles dry quickly so resist the growth of moisture-loving microbes.

USING WOOL

Fibres taken from the coats of sheep and other mammals can be used to make the group of natural materials we call wool. Nearly 60 km (37 miles) of fine woollen yarn can be made from 1 kg (2.2 lbs) of wool. This material is hard-wearing, warm, and resistant to water and microbes.

Bus seats are covered in hard-wearing woollen fabric.

BUS SEATS

YARN

Firefighters' protective gear and fire blankets contain wool, which is naturally resistant to fire.

FIREFIGHTERS' GEAR

SHEEP
Densely coated animals
Every year more than a billion sheep are sheared so that their thick wool coats can be spun into yarn. This yarn is then used to make fabrics and clothing.

BASEBALL LINING

About 200 m (656 ft) of wool yarn is wrapped around the ball's core.

HAT

FELT
This unwoven material is made from matted wool. Felt is used in crafts and in industry to dampen machinery noise and vibrations.

BUILDING INSULATION

CLOTHING

Wool mixed with recycled fibres keeps heat in and cold out.

HOME | 97

The hair of an Angora goat grows by 20–30 cm (8–12 in) each year.

GOATS
Animals with fine-fibred coats

Goats yield two types of wool. Fine cashmere forms the winter coat of the Kashmir goat, while thicker mohair comes from the Angora goat.

Many shawls, scarves, and sweaters are made of light, super-soft cashmere fibres.

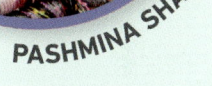
PASHMINA SHAWLS

Fine, lustrous mohair fibres are used to make knitted or woven clothing.

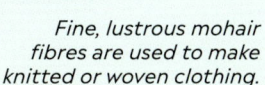
MOHAIR SCARF

ALPACA WOOL GLOVES

Llama produce thick, tough wool suitable for ropes, rugs, bags, and blankets.

LLAMA WOOL BAGS

SOUTH AMERICAN CAMELIDS
Soft-haired mammals

The wool of the alpaca (above), llama, vicuña, and guanaco tends to be softer than that of a sheep. The fibres of an alpaca's coat are hollow, which makes this animal's wool especially warm to wear.

VICUÑA WOOL COAT

Fine vicuña wool is used to make expensive luxury clothing.

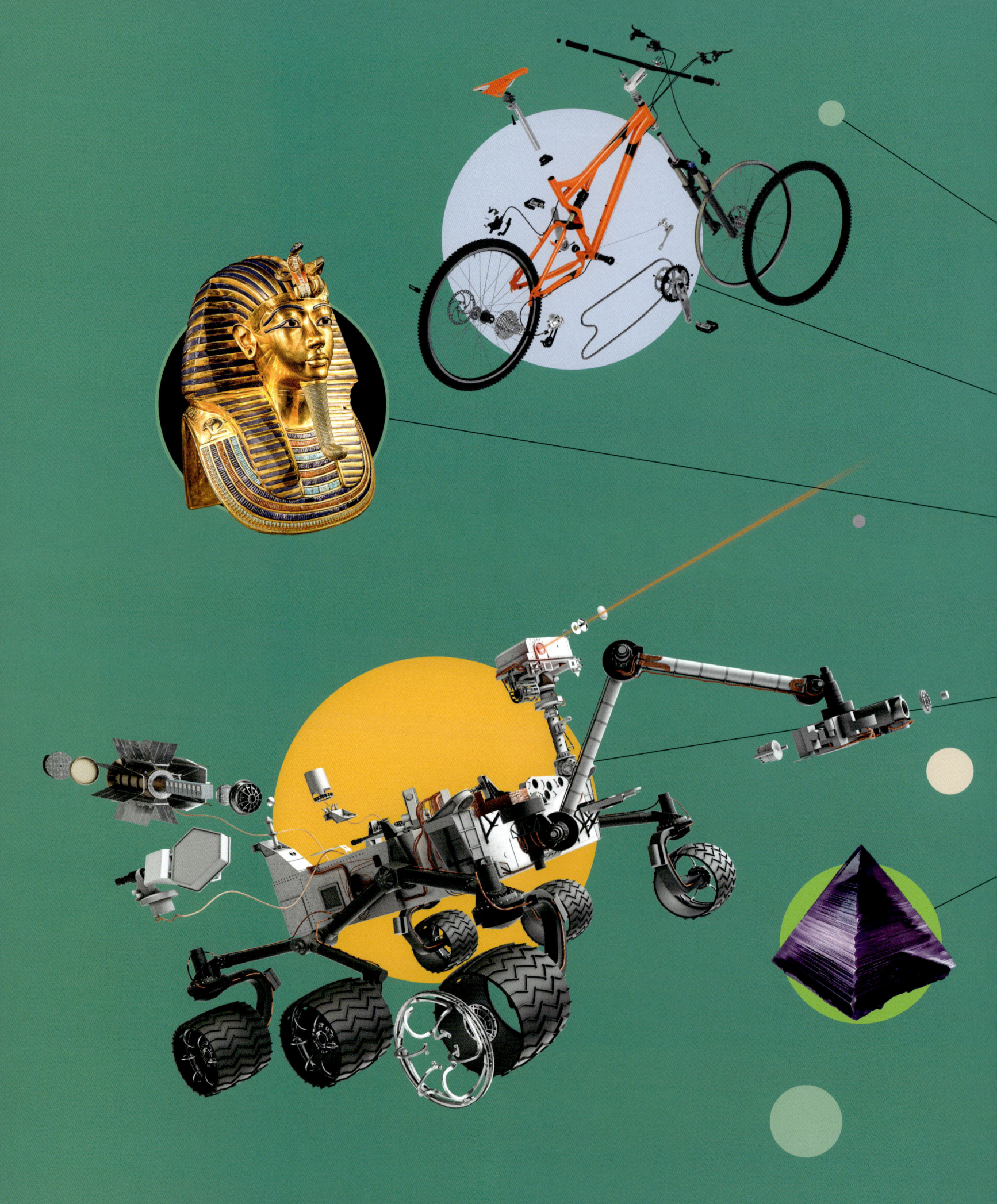

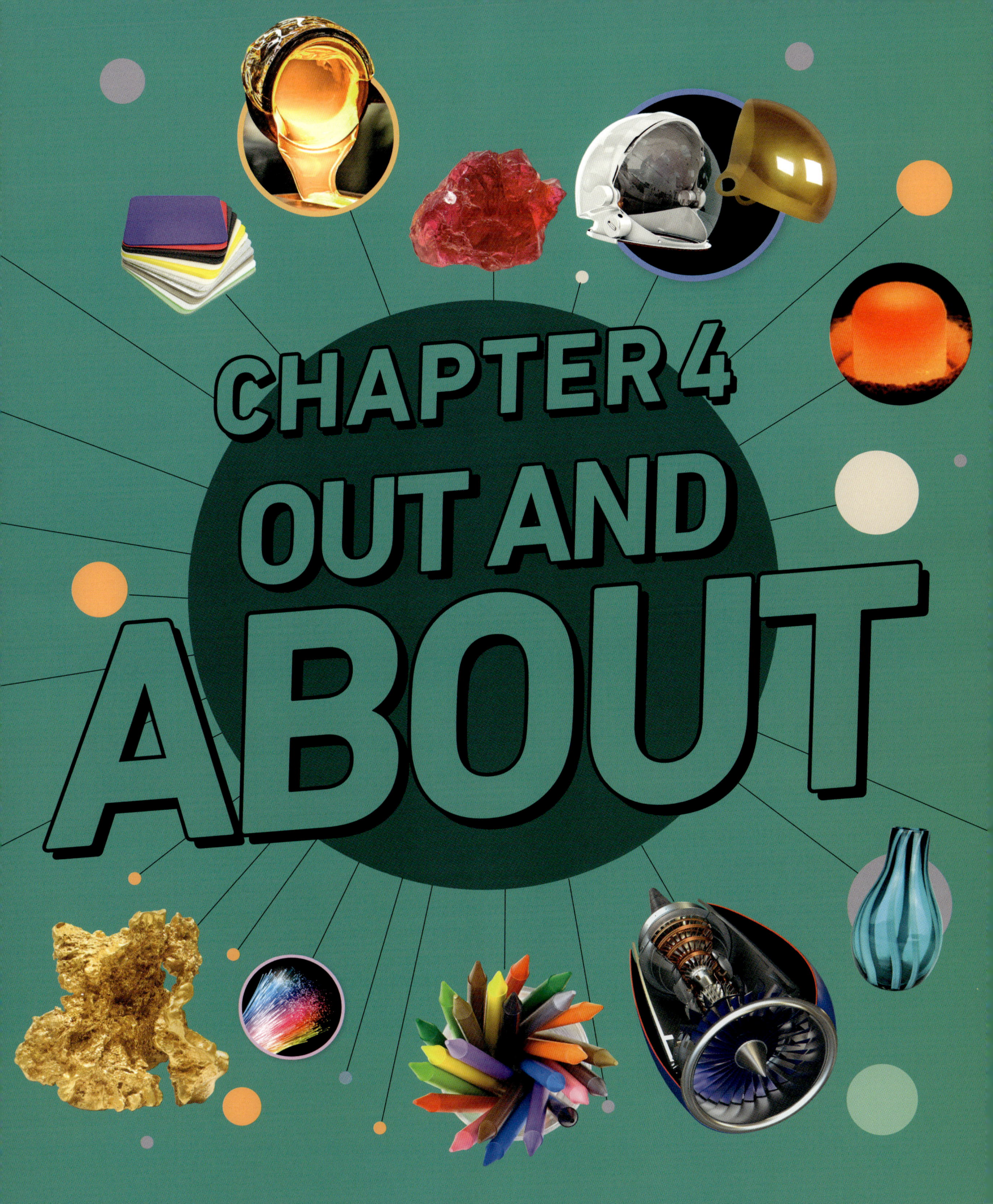

CHAPTER 4
OUT AND ABOUT

OUT AND ABOUT

SKIING

People have used skis to move on snow for thousands of years. Traditionally, skis were carved from single pieces of wood, but modern skis are made from layers of different materials glued together. Early ski boots were just leather winter boots tied to the skis. Modern boots are made from hard plastic and clip onto the skis.

THE OLDEST SKIS DISCOVERED ARE OVER 8,000 YEARS OLD.

Aluminium
High-quality ski bindings often contain aluminium alloy, a lightweight and tough metal.

Stainless steel
Hard stainless steel is wrapped around the edge of the ski, cutting into the ice and preventing the ski from slipping.

Hard plastic
Most ski boots are made with polyurethane – a cheap, elastic, and durable polymer.

Polyethylene
A smooth, lightweight plastic, polyethylene, is moulded to form the base.

LAMINATED WOOD
Strong and durable

The core of the ski is made from strips of laminated hardwood. The strips are laid out with the grains in different directions to reduce the risk of weaknesses causing breakages. The strips are then glued together.

WAX
Smooth coat that repels water

A hard, paraffin-based wax is applied to the base of a ski. The wax repels water – preventing it from building up between the skis and the snow – in order to reduce friction.

HOW IS IT MADE?

The first part of the ski to be made is the core – this involves glueing together dozens of thin layers of wood. Next, the core and other layers (including layers of fibreglass and carbon fibre composites) are glued together inside a mould, then heated and pressed. Finally, the ski is fitted with its remaining pieces and buffed, polished, decorated, and waxed.

- Top sheet
- Composite layer
- Laminated wood core
- Steel sidewall
- Composite layer
- Sidewall
- Rubber dampening strip
- Composite layer
- Steel edge
- Base

Rubber
Rubber is used in dampening strips that absorb vibrations as well as any sudden shocks from uneven ground while skiing.

EPOXY RESIN
Joins the layers

The skis are glued together with epoxy resin. This strong, synthetic adhesive hardens as it sets.

USING WATER

OUT AND ABOUT

Water is essential for life on Earth. It is the most used substance on the planet and a vital ingredient in many products, such as food, medicines, ceramics, and concrete. Water is also widely used as a cleaning agent, as well as a coolant and a solvent (a substance that dissolves things easily, to form mixtures).

HYDROGEN FUEL
Water can be split into oxygen and hydrogen, which powers some buses.

FOOD
Water is required to boil, poach, and steam food, and is also added to soups and sauces. It is injected into some meats to increase their weight.

SAUCES

Milk is treated with steam to remove harmful bacteria.

High-pressure steam turns the blades of a turbine, which powers a generator to produce electricity.

STEAM TURBINE GENERATOR

MILK PASTEURIZATION

WATER
Vital liquid

Water covers about 70 per cent of Earth's surface. This colourless, tasteless, and odourless liquid makes up around 55–60 per cent of an adult human's weight.

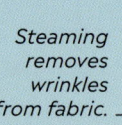

Steaming removes wrinkles from fabric.

STEAMING FABRICS

STEAM
Heating water changes it into steam. This hot gas kills bacteria, cooks food, and is also used to heat buildings and generate electricity.

OUT AND ABOUT | 103

INDUSTRIAL SOLVENT
Water is called the universal solvent as it dissolves more substances than any other liquid. It is used to dilute chemicals to make fertilizers, medicines, and more.

Adding water to pigments forms liquid paints.

PAINT

LEAD ACID BATTERIES

Distilled water is mixed with sulphuric acid to form a chemical paste that allows electricity to flow in a battery.

DISTILLED WATER
This is purified water made by boiling water, collecting the steam, and then cooling the gas back into a liquid. Distilled water is free of minerals and impurities, making it useful in labs and hospitals.

MEDICAL CLEANING

Surgeons and nurses use distilled water to clean their hands and steam medical instruments.

ICE
Ice is used to cool and preserve food, and in the chemicals industry to slow down or stop chemical reactions.

ICE SCULPTURE

Ice arches and walls at the Ice Hotel in Quebec, Canada

ICE BATH FOR CHEMICALS

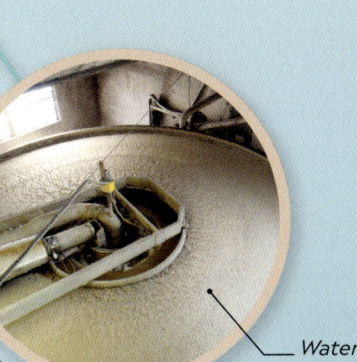

PAPER PULP

Water is added to wood pulp before the mix is pressed, rolled, and dried to make paper.

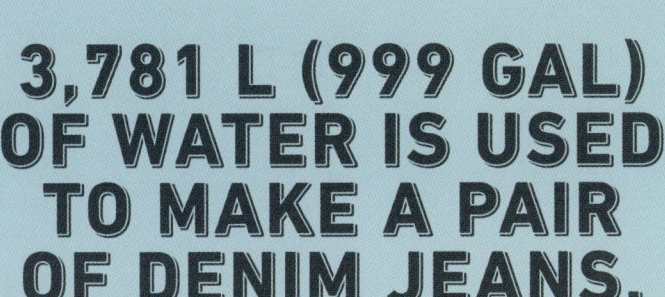

3,781 L (999 GAL) OF WATER IS USED TO MAKE A PAIR OF DENIM JEANS.

104 OUT AND ABOUT

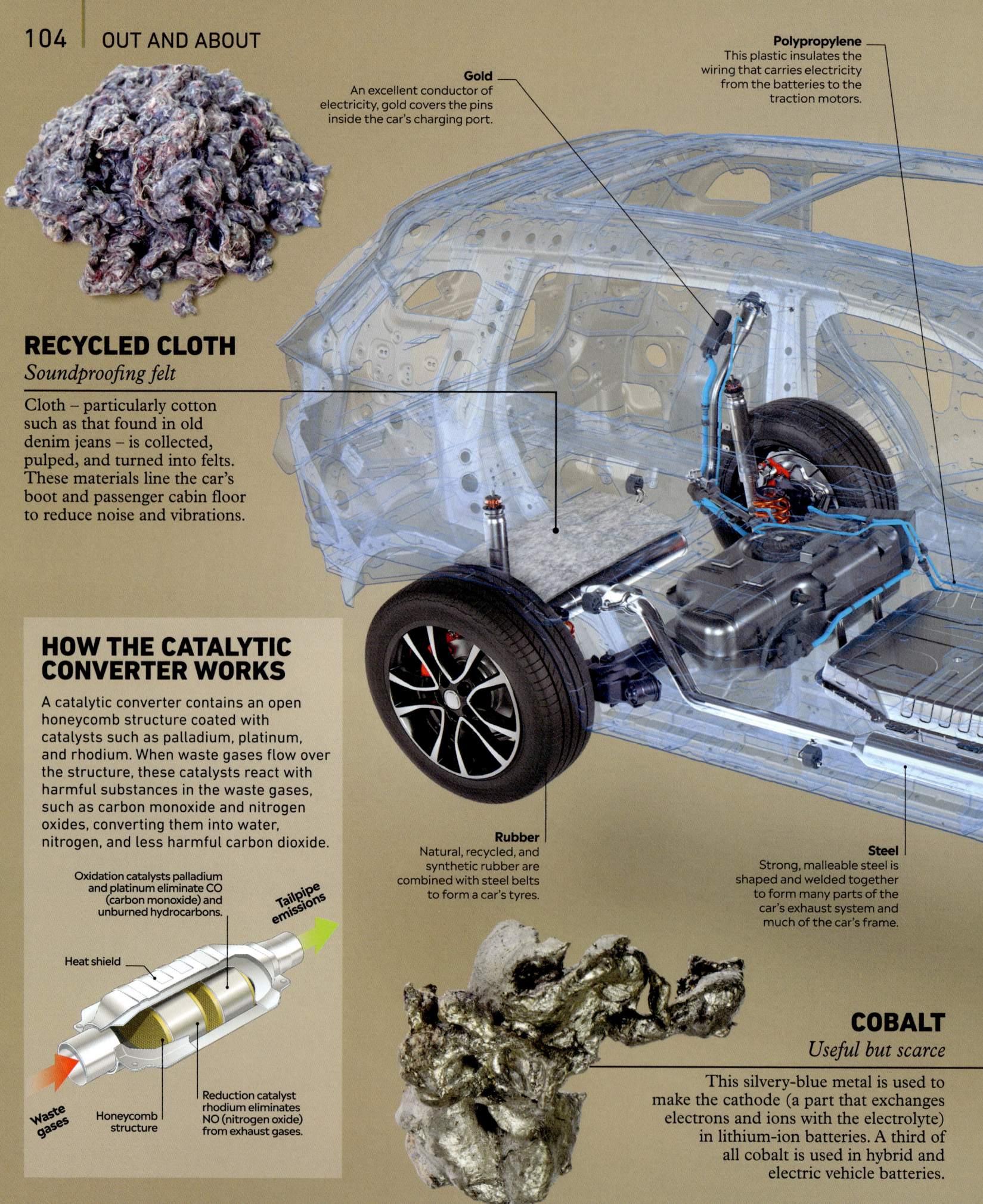

Gold
An excellent conductor of electricity, gold covers the pins inside the car's charging port.

Polypropylene
This plastic insulates the wiring that carries electricity from the batteries to the traction motors.

RECYCLED CLOTH
Soundproofing felt

Cloth – particularly cotton such as that found in old denim jeans – is collected, pulped, and turned into felts. These materials line the car's boot and passenger cabin floor to reduce noise and vibrations.

HOW THE CATALYTIC CONVERTER WORKS

A catalytic converter contains an open honeycomb structure coated with catalysts such as palladium, platinum, and rhodium. When waste gases flow over the structure, these catalysts react with harmful substances in the waste gases, such as carbon monoxide and nitrogen oxides, converting them into water, nitrogen, and less harmful carbon dioxide.

Oxidation catalysts palladium and platinum eliminate CO (carbon monoxide) and unburned hydrocarbons.

Tailpipe emissions

Heat shield

Waste gases

Honeycomb structure

Reduction catalyst rhodium eliminates NO (nitrogen oxide) from exhaust gases.

Rubber
Natural, recycled, and synthetic rubber are combined with steel belts to form a car's tyres.

Steel
Strong, malleable steel is shaped and welded together to form many parts of the car's exhaust system and much of the car's frame.

COBALT
Useful but scarce

This silvery-blue metal is used to make the cathode (a part that exchanges electrons and ions with the electrolyte) in lithium-ion batteries. A third of all cobalt is used in hybrid and electric vehicle batteries.

OUT AND ABOUT | 105

HYBRID SUV CAR

Plug-in hybrid cars have not one, but two power systems: a compact internal combustion engine using petrol as fuel, and a large lithium-ion battery pack powering electric traction motors that turn the car's wheels. The battery pack can be recharged by plugging it into a mains electricity supply. Using electricity in this way reduces fuel consumption and lowers carbon emissions.

PVB
The plastic polyvinyl butyral (PVB) is sandwiched between glass layers to form tough, safe laminated glass for car windscreens.

The steering wheel has a cushioning layer of polyurethane foam covered by a plastic vinyl or leather.

Ferrovanadium
Suspension springs made of this alloy of iron and vanadium absorb forces when the vehicle travels over bumps and dips.

EPDM
Ethylene Propylene Diene Monomer (EPDM) synthetic rubber hoses circulate liquid coolant to cool the traction motors.

Dysprosium
This rare-earth metal is used to make powerful permanent magnets inside the car's electric motors.

The catalytic converter is fitted to the exhaust system to treat waste gases from the engine.

NUT SHELLS
Friction generators
Resin from ground-up nut shells, along with graphite, powdered metals, and rubber granules, is used to form rough-surfaced brake pads. When pressed onto the brake disc, the pads grip and generate friction, slowing the wheel down.

OUT AND ABOUT

GUANIDINE NITRATE
A powerful propellant

Modern airbags are inflated by a chemical reaction that uses a salt called guanidine nitrate. When it is heated, this salt rapidly decomposes, releasing water, carbon, and a huge amount of nitrogen gas, which inflates the airbag.

Sensor detects when the car stops suddenly.

Igniter

Stainless steel
A stainless steel filter surrounds the pellets of guanidine nitrate.

Storage area behind the steering wheel where the folded-up bag is stored.

CAR AIRBAG

Since 1998, all cars must have at least two airbags – one for the driver and one for the front-seat passenger. In an impact, the airbag fills almost instantaneously with gas, forming a protective cushion that reduces the risk of passenger injury.

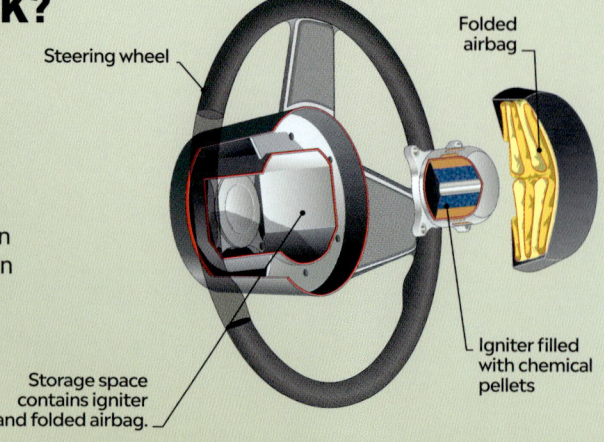

CORN FLOUR
Non-stick powder

The airbag is coated with corn flour or talcum powder before being folded up inside the steering wheel. This powder absorbs moisture to stop the cushion's surfaces sticking together.

HOW DOES IT WORK?

During a crash, a sensor in the front of the car is triggered and sends an electric signal to the igniter (a tiny explosive charge). The heat from the igniter begins a chemical reaction, causing the cushion to fill with nitrogen gas in 15–30 milliseconds, depending on the force of impact. The driver or passenger then hits the cushion instead of the car interior.

Steering wheel

Folded airbag

Storage space contains igniter and folded airbag.

Igniter filled with chemical pellets

OUT AND ABOUT | 107

MODERN CARS CAN HAVE AS MANY AS 10 AIRBAGS.

NYLON 6,6
Strong and stable yarn

The cushion fabric is made from nylon 6,6 yarn, which is exceptionally strong and fire-resistant. The yarn is made by pushing a type of liquid plastic through tiny holes, then stretching, twisting, and winding it onto spools. The fabric is then woven on a computerized loom.

The airbag housing is mounted on the steering wheel.

Nitrogen gas
The nitrogen gas filling the cushion is inert, which means it is safe and won't react any further.

Silicone rubber
The airbag is spray-coated with silicone rubber to ensure no gas escapes.

MOUNTAIN BIKE

A bicycle is a small vehicle that moves when a rider, seated on the saddle, pushes on the pedals. Mountain bikes have powerful brakes, a strong frame, and wider tyres than regular bikes to help them travel across rough, uneven terrain.

SYNTHETIC MICA
Protective sheen

The mineral mica has a natural shine when powdered. Synthetic mica is made in labs and mimics the shimmery quality of natural mica. It is added to vehicle paint to make it more vibrant and reflective. Synthetic mica also protects metal from corrosion.

THE WORLD'S LONGEST BIKE IS 55.16 M (180.97 FT).

Nylon is used for the saddle because it is lightweight and can be easily moulded into a comfortable shape.

Brake disc

Steel chain transfers the crank's motion to the rear wheel as the rider pedals.

Rubber
The tyre tread is made of rubber, which is easily shaped, "grippy", and absorbs impact well.

Gear-changing device (the cassette) is made of steel.

OUT AND ABOUT | 109

CARBON FIBRE COMPOSITE
Stronger than steel

The frames of high-end bicycles are often made of a composite material containing carbon fibre. This lightweight material is rigid, strong, and resistant to corrosion.

Silicone
This soft material is used for the handlebar grips as it is comfortable to grasp for long periods.

CROSS-COUNTRY MOUNTAIN BIKING BECAME AN OLYMPIC SPORT IN 1996.

Stainless steel
Many parts of the bike, including the spokes, chain, and cassette, are made of this durable metal.

Crank

Pedal

CARBON BLACK
Toughening powder

This fine black powder is pure carbon, produced from burning wood and petroleum products. Carbon black is added to the rubber used for tyres, to make them stiff and wear-resistant. It also gives tyres their distinctive black colour.

110 OUT AND ABOUT

USING GLASS

From the largest window pane to the tiniest lens, glass helps us see the world. It is easily manufactured from ingredients that are abundant in nature, and made stronger or more colourful by adding small amounts of chemicals. This versatile material is also waterproof, and a good insulator against heat and electricity.

HOW IS IT MADE?

To make glass, raw materials are heated at very high temperatures until they soften to form a transparent liquid that can be easily moulded or stretched. Once the liquid glass has been shaped, it is cooled slowly to make it less likely to fracture or shatter.

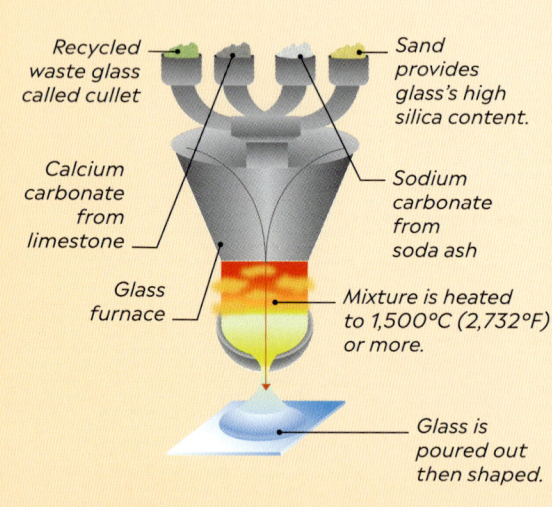

- Recycled waste glass called cullet
- Sand provides glass's high silica content.
- Calcium carbonate from limestone
- Sodium carbonate from soda ash
- Glass furnace
- Mixture is heated to 1,500°C (2,732°F) or more.
- Glass is poured out then shaped.

GLASS CAN BE RECYCLED ENDLESSLY.

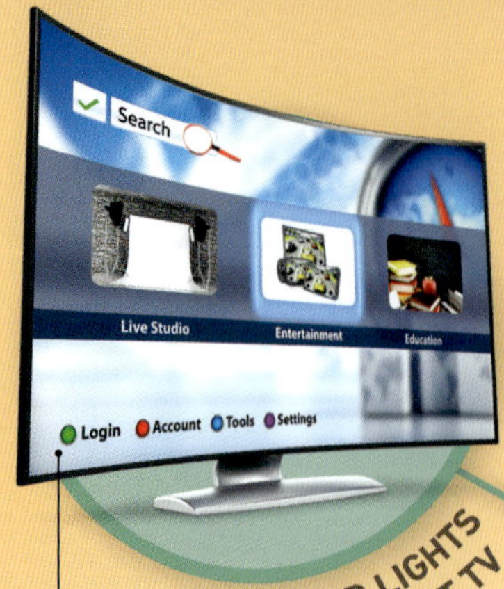

OLED LIGHTS IN SMART TV
Screen made up of thousands of tiny OLED lights mounted on borosilicate glass.

BOROSILICATE GLASS
Mixed with the chemical compound boron trioxide, this durable glass can tolerate sudden changes of temperature better than regular glass. It is often used to make laboratory glassware.

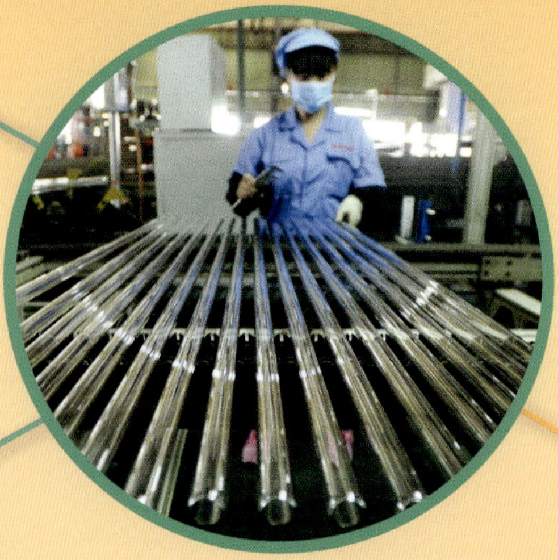

COOKWARE AND BAKEWARE

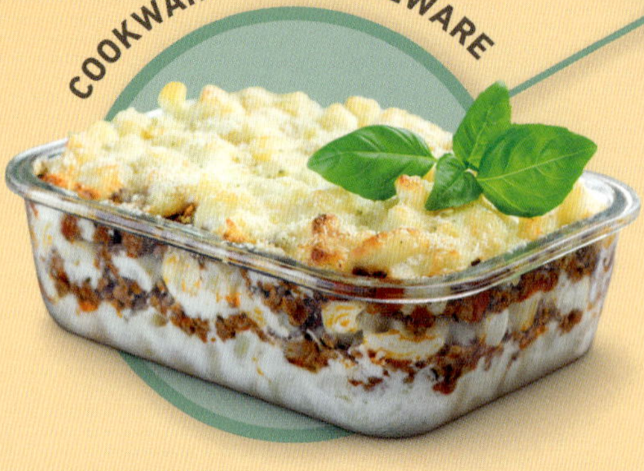

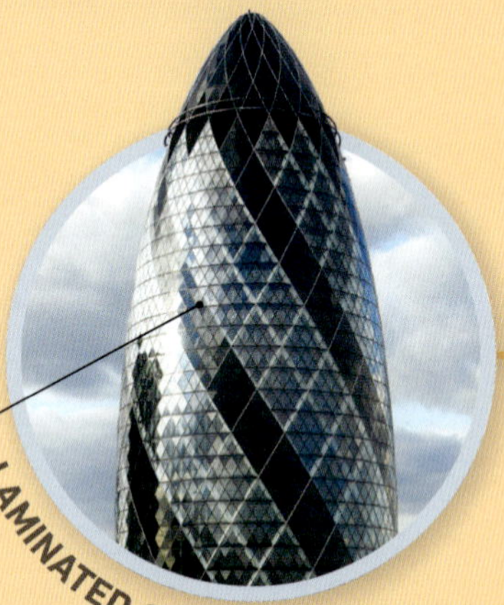

SPECTACLE LENSES

LAMINATED GLASS
Double-pane glass windows of this building in London, UK, keep out UV radiation.

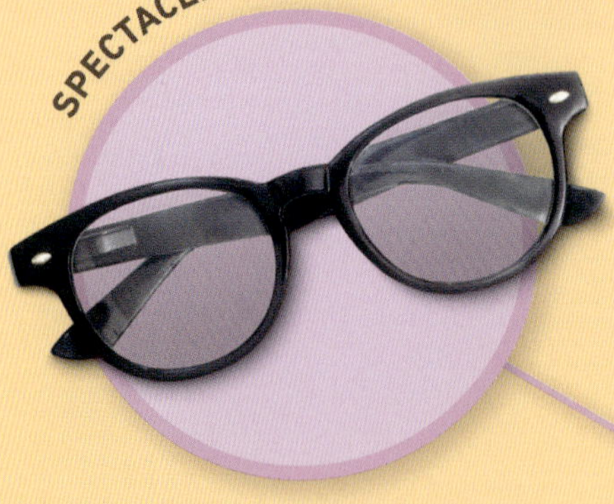

FIBRE-OPTIC CABLES
Fibre-optic cables enable data signals to travel extremely fast.

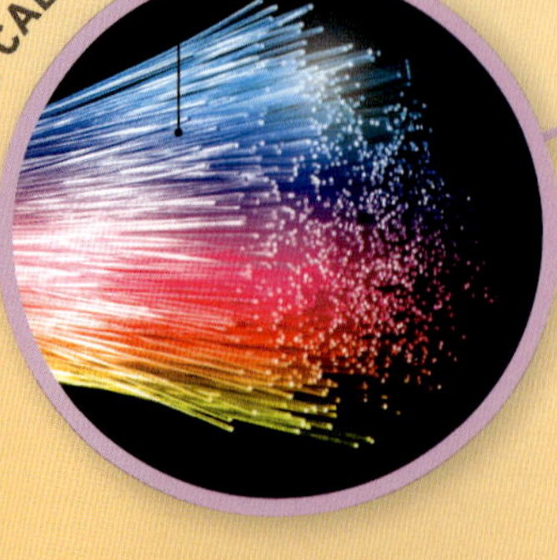

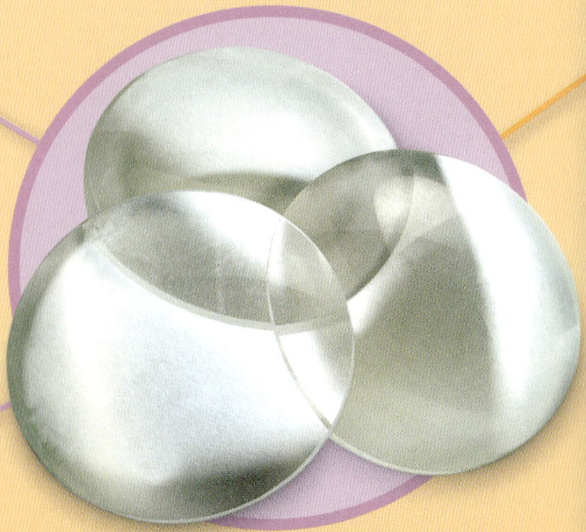

SILICA GLASS
Made almost entirely of pure silica, this specialty glass is tough and completely transparent. It is formed into fine strands for fibre optic cables and used in spacecraft windows, lenses, and lasers.

OUT AND ABOUT | 111

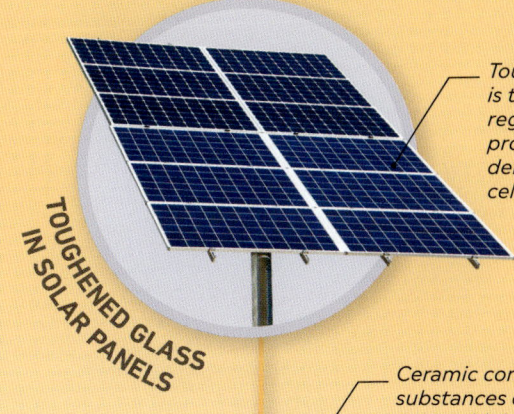
Toughened glass is tougher than regular glass and protects the delicate solar cells beneath.

TOUGHENED GLASS IN SOLAR PANELS

LIGHT BULB

Coloured glass is made by adding metallic oxide powders to liquid glass.

GLASSWARE

Ceramic container in which substances can be heated at very high temperatures.

Liquid glass flows as it is poured onto a bath of molten tin.

SODA-LIME GLASS

From transparent or coloured to scratch-resistant or toughened, more than three-quarters of all glass produced in the world is soda-lime glass. It is used in many everyday items such as jewellery, mirrors, windows, and jars.

Frosted or patterned glass lets some light in while maintaining privacy.

OBSCURE GLASS

GLASS FIBRE

This lightweight material is made up of fine glass fibres. It is easily moulded into various shapes, does not rot, and is a great insulator of heat and electricity.

LIQUID GLASS
Mouldable mixture

Heating limestone, sand, and soda ash to high temperatures creates liquid glass. Before it cools down, this liquid is poured into moulds and either blown to form different objects, or floated on large vats or baths of molten tin to form perfectly flat sheets of glass.

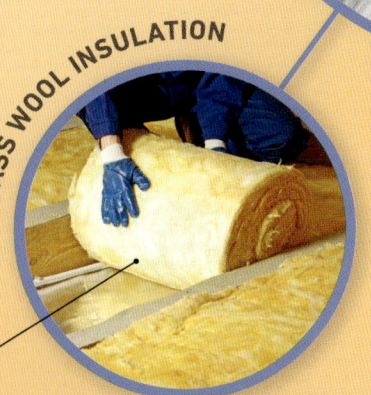

GLASS WOOL INSULATION

A thick layer of glass wool insulation in the roof space traps heat inside buildings in winter.

FIBREGLASS-REINFORCED SNOWBOARD

Fibreglass provides stiffness to snowboards, and keeps them from deforming under pressure.

OUT AND ABOUT

MAGNESIUM ALLOY
Light and strong

This durable alloy is stiff and strong and its light weight makes the binoculars more comfortable to hold for long periods. The material also doesn't expand or contract in hot or cold conditions.

This knob adjusts focus by altering the distance between the eyepiece lens and objective lens.

GUTTA-PERCHA
Tough and textured

This natural latex rubber obtained from Malaysia's gutta-percha tree provides a hardwearing outer coating. It also gives a textured feel to the exterior, making the binoculars easier to grip.

ABS plastic
The eye cup is moulded from a hard plastic called Acrylonitrile Butadiene Styrene (ABS).

A central hinge allows the two barrels to be moved closer together or further apart to match the distance between a person's eyes.

BINOCULARS

Using side-by-side lenses in barrels, binoculars make distant objects, from birds and boats to planets and galaxies in the night sky, much bigger. Binoculars are carefully designed to minimize reflections, which can reduce the clarity of the magnified image.

The right eyepiece can be focused independently of the central focus knob. This is to allow for differences in sight between a person's two eyes.

Borosilicate glass
Triangular prisms made from glass made up of silica and boron trioxide allow more light to reach the eyepiece than ordinary glass or plastics.

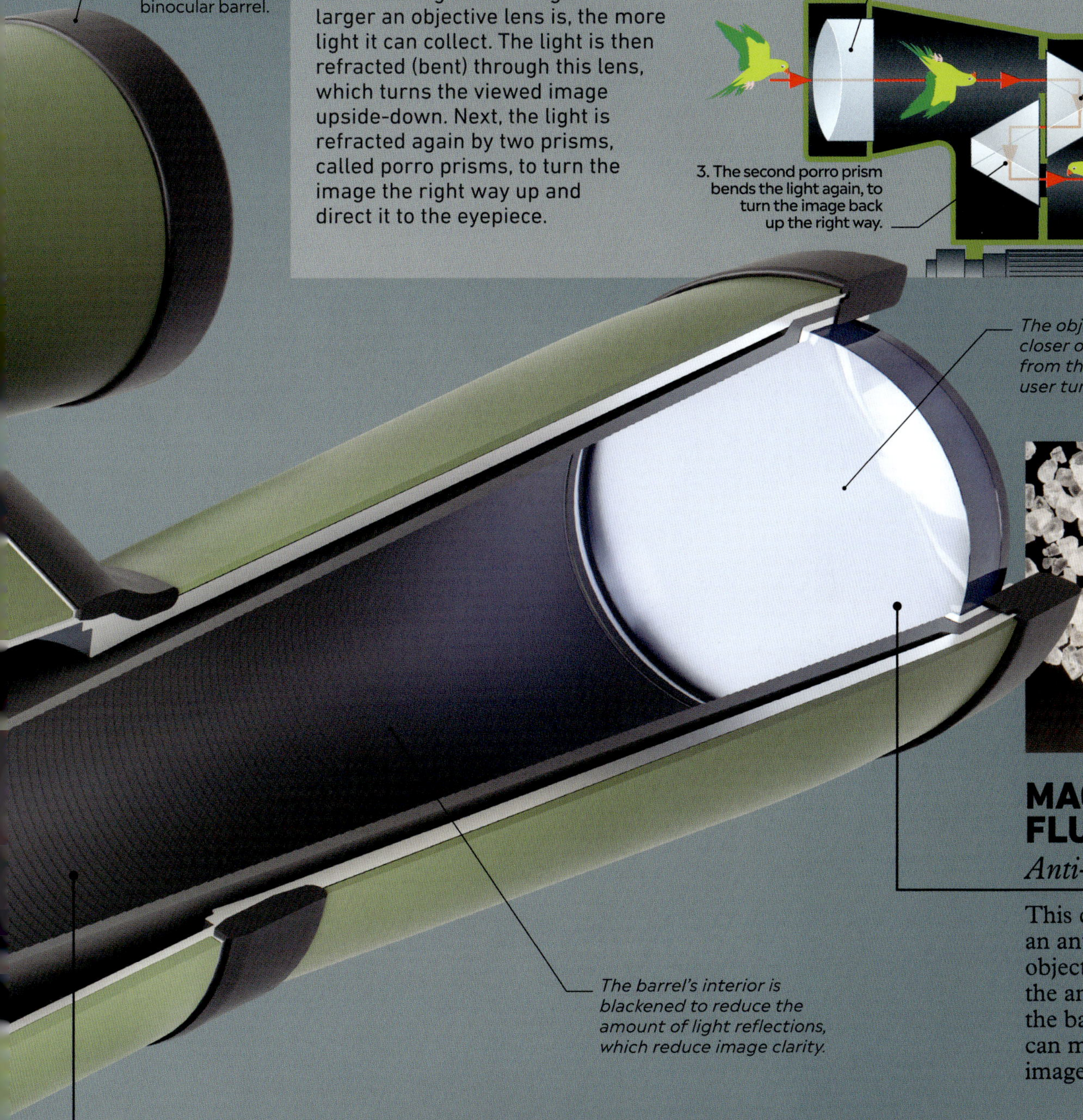

OUT AND ABOUT | 113

Synthetic rubber
A rubber seal stops moisture or air from entering each binocular barrel.

HOW DOES IT WORK?

The objective lens at the front of each barrel gathers in light. The larger an objective lens is, the more light it can collect. The light is then refracted (bent) through this lens, which turns the viewed image upside-down. Next, the light is refracted again by two prisms, called porro prisms, to turn the image the right way up and direct it to the eyepiece.

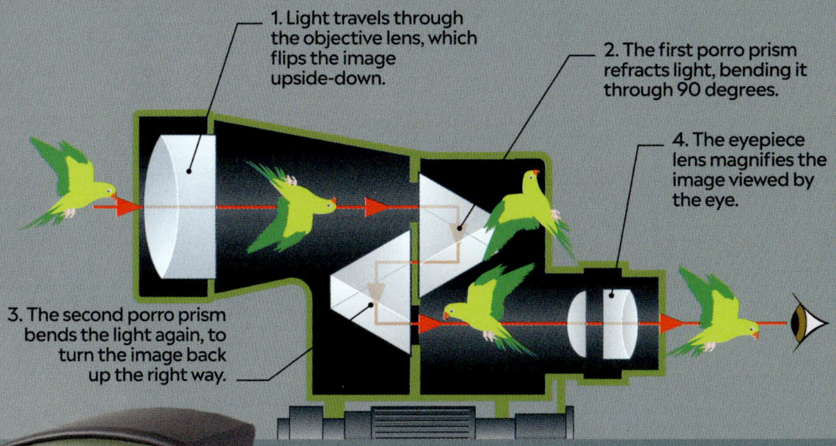

1. Light travels through the objective lens, which flips the image upside-down.

2. The first porro prism refracts light, bending it through 90 degrees.

3. The second porro prism bends the light again, to turn the image back up the right way.

4. The eyepiece lens magnifies the image viewed by the eye.

The objective lens moves closer or further away from the eyepiece as the user turns the focus knob.

The barrel's interior is blackened to reduce the amount of light reflections, which reduce image clarity.

MAGNESIUM FLUORIDE
Anti-reflective

This crystal compound forms an anti-reflective coating on the objective lens. The coating increases the amount of light gathered into the barrel by 3–5 per cent, which can make a big difference to image clarity.

NITROGEN GAS
Cleansing gas

The barrels of good-quality binoculars are injected with nitrogen gas. This "purges" their interior, removing any air that might contain moisture that would cause the glass lenses to fog and turn cloudy.

LUNAR CRATERS JUST 10 KM (6 MILES) WIDE CAN BE SEEN WITH BINOCULARS.

OUT AND ABOUT
USING PETROLEUM

Petroleum, or crude oil, is a fossil fuel and an important non-renewable natural resource. It powers our world, providing fuel for transport and raw materials for many industries. Petroleum is used to make a range of products, such as gasoline, lubricants, and plastics.

Liquefied petroleum gas (LPG) is used as cooking gas in many countries as it is easy to store and transport.

LPG

GASOLINE

FUEL
Petroleum fuels generate large amounts of energy when burned. About 45 per cent of all petroleum is refined to make gasoline, which fuels motor vehicles and some electricity generators.

Jet fuels generate more energy than gasoline, and can be designed to withstand harsh weather.

AVIATION FUEL

LUBRICANTS

PARAFFIN WAX
This white, odourless wax is used in cosmetics and medical ointments because it can retain moisture and form a protective barrier for the skin. It is also a good lubricant and is added to mechanical grease.

CRAYONS

Paraffin wax burns evenly.

CANDLE

REFINED PETROLEUM
Fossil fuel

Found in underground rock formations, petroleum is created when plant and animal remains are transformed by heat and pressure over millions of years. It is extracted (often by pumps, as above) and processed at high temperatures to produce different products.

OUT AND ABOUT | 115

PETROLEUM JELLY
A blend of mineral oils and natural wax, petroleum jelly is an effective moisturizer and lubricant, and can help wounds to heal. It is used in many skin creams and lip balms.

PLASTICINE

Modelling clay contains some petroleum jelly to keep it soft and pliable.

POLYPROPYLENE

Strong, tough, waterproof plastic

NAPHTHA
Naphtha is a flammable liquid often extracted from petroleum. It is used as a solvent in paints and varnishes, and to make many plastics including polyethylene foam (right).

POLYSTYRENE

Polystyrene, a lightweight packing material, is made from naphtha.

Bitumen acts as a binder in asphalt, keeping the aggregate materials together.

BUTYL RUBBER

Butyl, a synthetic rubber made from naphtha, provides an elastic and chewy base for many chewing gums.

Rolls of bitumen-based felt are used to line roofs.

ASPHALT

BITUMEN
This thick, sticky substance is a flexible building material that produces durable and weather-resistant products. It forms the rubbery backing of carpet tiles and is used to make waterproof roofing material and roof tiles.

HOW IS PETROLEUM EXTRACTED?
When a reservoir of petroleum is found beneath dry land or the seabed, a deep well is drilled into the ground to reach it. The oil may naturally rise to the surface due to the pressure in the rock formations, but if not it is pumped out and transported to a refinery.

Pump

Oil flows to the well head.

Oil reservoir within layers of rock formation

Extracting petroleum

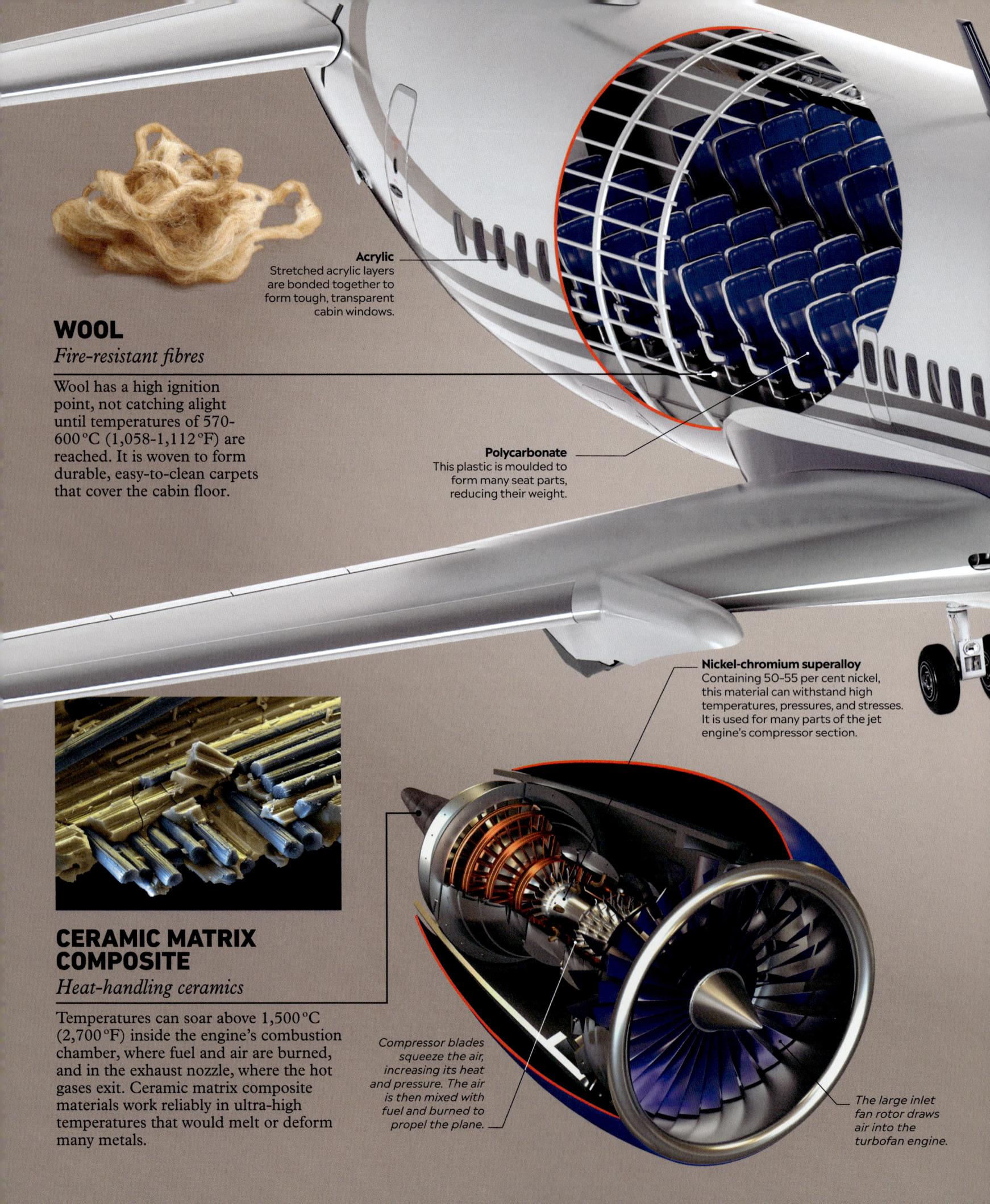

Acrylic
Stretched acrylic layers are bonded together to form tough, transparent cabin windows.

WOOL
Fire-resistant fibres

Wool has a high ignition point, not catching alight until temperatures of 570-600 °C (1,058-1,112 °F) are reached. It is woven to form durable, easy-to-clean carpets that cover the cabin floor.

Polycarbonate
This plastic is moulded to form many seat parts, reducing their weight.

Nickel-chromium superalloy
Containing 50-55 per cent nickel, this material can withstand high temperatures, pressures, and stresses. It is used for many parts of the jet engine's compressor section.

CERAMIC MATRIX COMPOSITE
Heat-handling ceramics

Temperatures can soar above 1,500 °C (2,700 °F) inside the engine's combustion chamber, where fuel and air are burned, and in the exhaust nozzle, where the hot gases exit. Ceramic matrix composite materials work reliably in ultra-high temperatures that would melt or deform many metals.

Compressor blades squeeze the air, increasing its heat and pressure. The air is then mixed with fuel and burned to propel the plane.

The large inlet fan rotor draws air into the turbofan engine.

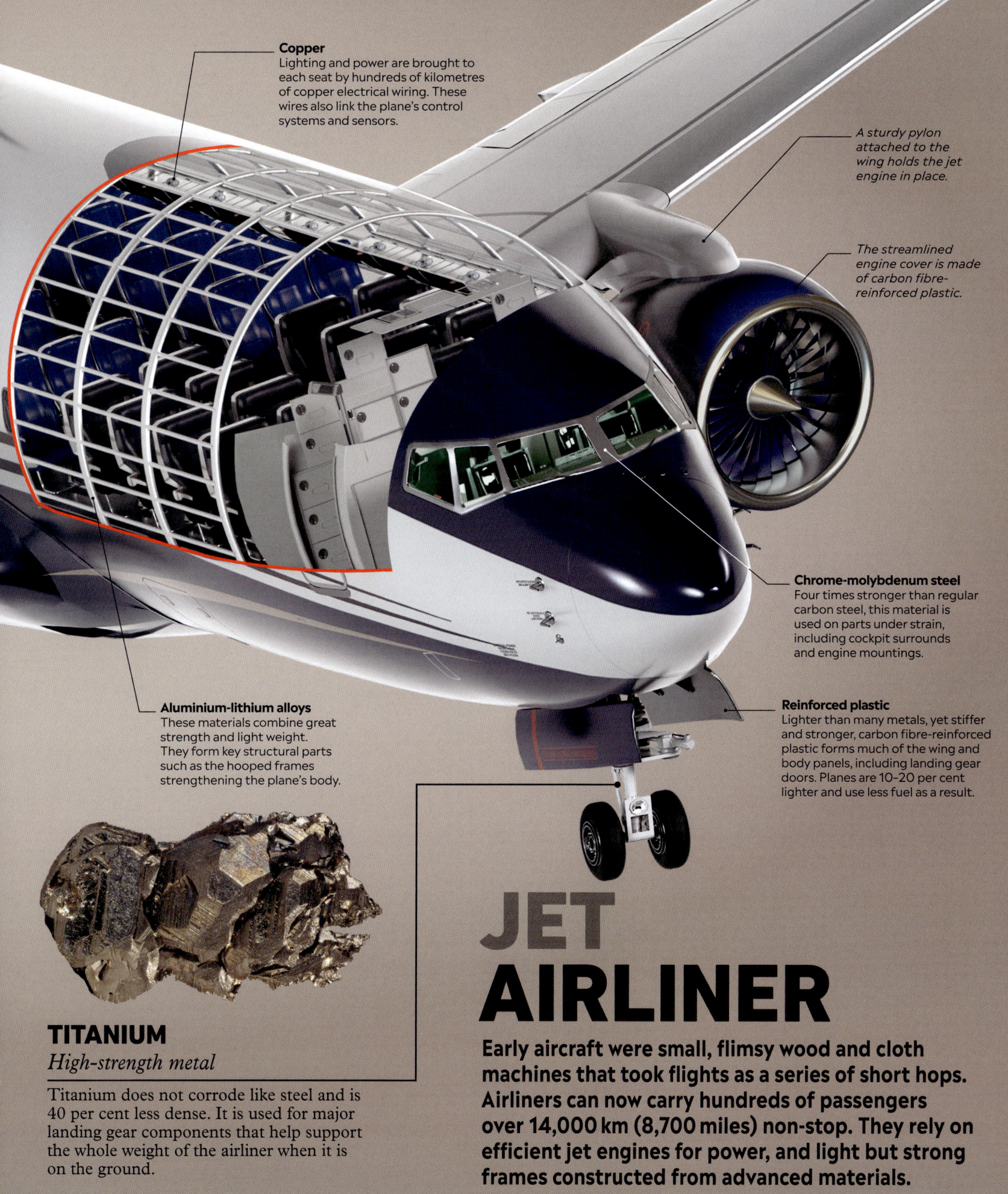

Copper
Lighting and power are brought to each seat by hundreds of kilometres of copper electrical wiring. These wires also link the plane's control systems and sensors.

A sturdy pylon attached to the wing holds the jet engine in place.

The streamlined engine cover is made of carbon fibre-reinforced plastic.

Chrome-molybdenum steel
Four times stronger than regular carbon steel, this material is used on parts under strain, including cockpit surrounds and engine mountings.

Aluminium-lithium alloys
These materials combine great strength and light weight. They form key structural parts such as the hooped frames strengthening the plane's body.

Reinforced plastic
Lighter than many metals, yet stiffer and stronger, carbon fibre-reinforced plastic forms much of the wing and body panels, including landing gear doors. Planes are 10–20 per cent lighter and use less fuel as a result.

TITANIUM
High-strength metal

Titanium does not corrode like steel and is 40 per cent less dense. It is used for major landing gear components that help support the whole weight of the airliner when it is on the ground.

JET AIRLINER

Early aircraft were small, flimsy wood and cloth machines that took flights as a series of short hops. Airliners can now carry hundreds of passengers over 14,000 km (8,700 miles) non-stop. They rely on efficient jet engines for power, and light but strong frames constructed from advanced materials.

118 OUT AND ABOUT

FIRE EXTINGUISHER

There are many types of fire extinguisher. Each contains a different material, such as water, powdered chemical, or foam, to put out a different type of fire. For example, water is used to put out flames on materials such as wood, paper, or clothing, while foam-based extinguishers are used to fight fires caused by flammable liquids, such as gasoline.

THE FIRST FIRE EXTINGUISHERS CONTAINED GUNPOWDER.

TYPES OF EXTINGUISHER

A fire requires heat, oxygen, and fuel to keep burning. Fire extinguishers work by cutting off the heat, oxygen, or both, to put out the fire. They do this by covering the fire with a cooling material that blocks contact with the air, cutting off the fire's supply of oxygen.

Water
Cools the surface and prevents the fire from continuing to burn

Foam
Forms a seal over the fuel, isolating it from oxygen

CO_2
Lowers the temperature and blocks the flow of oxygen

Powder
Forms a dry "blanket" of powder over the fire, blocking oxygen

Chemical
Sprays salts over the fire to create a film that cools and smothers it

OUT AND ABOUT

FOAM
Smothers fire

Aqueous film-forming foam (AFFF) is a fire-extinguishing substance made from water and foaming agents, such as sodium alkyl sulphate. When sprayed, it spreads quickly, puts out the flames, and prevents the fire from reigniting.

Plastic
Nozzles on foam-based extinguishers are usually made of lightweight plastic, which is resistant to corrosion and helps create an even spray.

A separate container holds the foaming agent away from the water, until the mixture can be discharged from the nozzle.

Reflective tape on a firefighter's clothing keeps them visible in smoke-filled spaces.

HOW DOES IT WORK?

AFFF extinguishers dispense a water-based foam that covers a fire. The water forms a cooling layer and lowers the temperature as it evaporates in contact with the flames. The foam creates a heat-resistant film over the flammable liquid, which keeps the oxygen out and "suffocates" the fire. The foam coating also ensures that the fire does not reignite.

Water vapour from the AFFF brings the temperature down.

Foam layer coats the fuel to keep oxygen out.

Fire • Foam • Fuel

Rubber
Reinforced, flexible rubber is used for the fire hose. This tough material is heat-resistant, does not react with chemicals easily, and can withstand the high pressures as the water flows through it.

Water travels through the rubber hose at a high pressure.

USING CEMENT AND CONCRETE

A fine powder called cement can be mixed with water and other substances to create concrete, the world's most used building material. Cement can also be used as a paste that sets hard to bind other building materials. Every year more than 4 billion tonnes of cement is produced globally to construct buildings, roads, bridges, and more.

CAST CONCRETE
Concrete can be poured into moulds to create statues and ornaments.

CEMENT
Binding agent
Limestone and clay are heated in an oven to form a lumpy material called clinker. Once cooled, the clinker and small quantities of the mineral gypsum are ground together to make cement. When cement is mixed with water and aggregate materials such as sand, it forms concrete.

REINFORCED CONCRETE
Concrete is embedded with steel bars (rebar), steel mesh, or glass fibres to strengthen or reinforce it. This prevents it from developing cracks, and allows it to support greater loads. Reinforced concrete is commonly used for the foundations of buildings.

FOUNDATIONS

Malaysia's Petronas Towers, the world's tallest twin structures, stand on 120 m- (394 ft-) deep reinforced concrete foundations.

MORTAR

Cement is mixed with sand and water to make a sticky paste that can be used to bind bricks.

STUCCO PLASTER
Made from cement, water, and limestone, stucco is a weather-resistant material used to decorate exterior walls.

ROADS

Concrete is used to create hard, even layers under the asphalt surfaces of roads.

OUT AND ABOUT | 121

CONCRETE DAM

The 221 m- (726 ft-) high Hoover Dam in Arizona, US, is made of concrete.

RECYCLED CONCRETE

Concrete rubble from demolition sites is crushed, sorted, and cleaned to produce stony chunks or chips for construction and landscaping. It is also used as aggregate to make fresh concrete.

Railway tracks are layered with concrete chips, called ballast, for support and stability.

BALLAST

Gabions are steel-mesh cages containing chunks of recycled concrete.

GABIONS

Sturdy pre-cast concrete rings are used to build the inner layers of tunnels.

TUNNEL RINGS

PRE-CAST CONCRETE

Concrete can be cast into different shapes at a factory and then transported to where it's needed. Common pre-cast parts include beams for buildings and slabs for pavements.

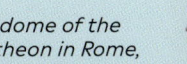

The dome of the Pantheon in Rome, Italy, was built in the 2nd century CE with concrete containing volcanic ash.

ROMAN CONCRETE

About 4,000 pre-cast panels were used in the roof of the Sydney Opera House, Australia.

ROOF PANELS

Concrete blocks placed along coastlines reduce the impact of strong waves.

COASTAL DEFENCES

CONCRETE CAN BE FIREPROOF AND WATERPROOF.

SHIP LOCK

The Three Gorges Dam on the Yangtze River in China is the world's largest concrete structure. Beside the dam are passageways with walls of reinforced concrete that allow ships to pass the dam safely. The passages contain long chambers, called ship locks, that fill with water when their large steel doors are opened. Here, workers are seen cleaning the chamber near one of the 280-m (920-ft) tall ship lock doors.

OUT AND ABOUT

WOOD COMPOSITE
Wood plus plastic

Long, thin threads called filaments that are malleable when heated are the main "ingredient" in 3D printing. In wood composite filament, a base of PLA (polylactic acid, a thermoplastic) is mixed with wood dust and cork. The wood only makes up around a third of the filament, but this is enough to give the finished product a wood-like appearance.

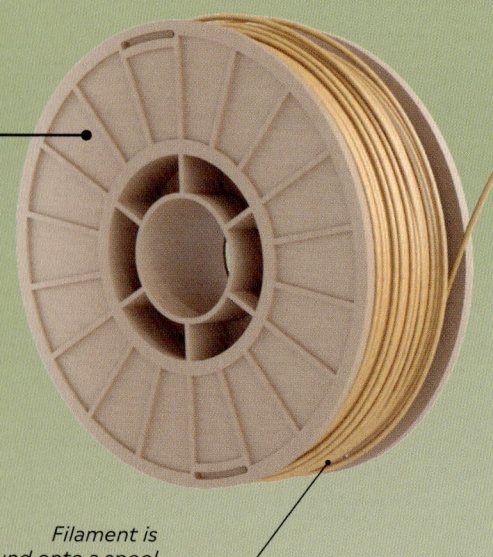

Filament is wound onto a spool for easy storage and dispensing.

3D PRINTER

Just as an ordinary printer can create a two-dimensional reproduction of an image, a 3D printer can create a three-dimensional copy of a digital model. 3D printers use different processes, but the most common machine works by building up thin layers of a material, such as molten plastic or wood composite, one on top of another.

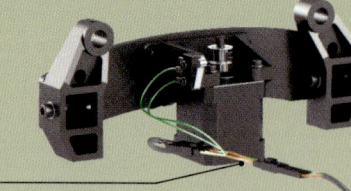

Copper
Copper wire is an excellent conductor of electricity.

Motherboard sends instructions from computer to printer.

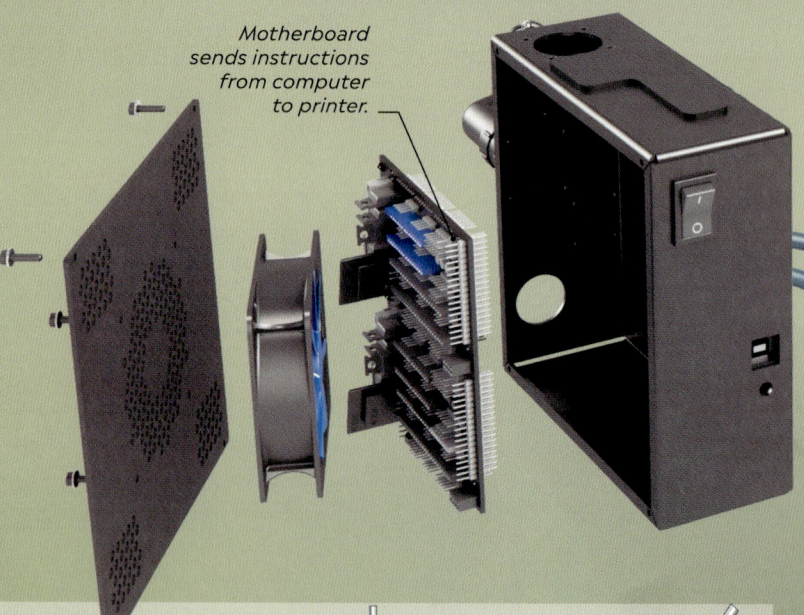

THE FIRST FULLY 3D-PRINTED PROSTHETIC EYE WAS GIVEN TO A PATIENT IN LONDON IN 2021.

HOW DOES IT WORK?

First, instructions about the shape and dimensions of the digital model are sent from a computer to the 3D printer. A thin, flexible filament is then fed through a hot nozzle in the printhead, which moves over the print bed, building up the 3D model layer by layer.

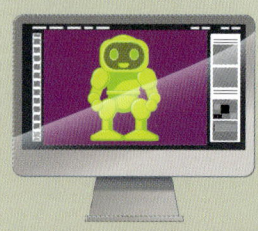

1. A 3D model is created using computer-aided design (CAD) software.

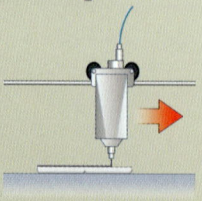

2. The printhead moves, laying down filament based on the design.

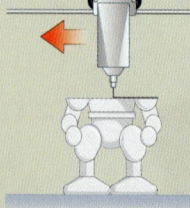

3. As the layers solidify more layers are built up on top of them.

4. The 3D object is finished by sanding and spraying as desired.

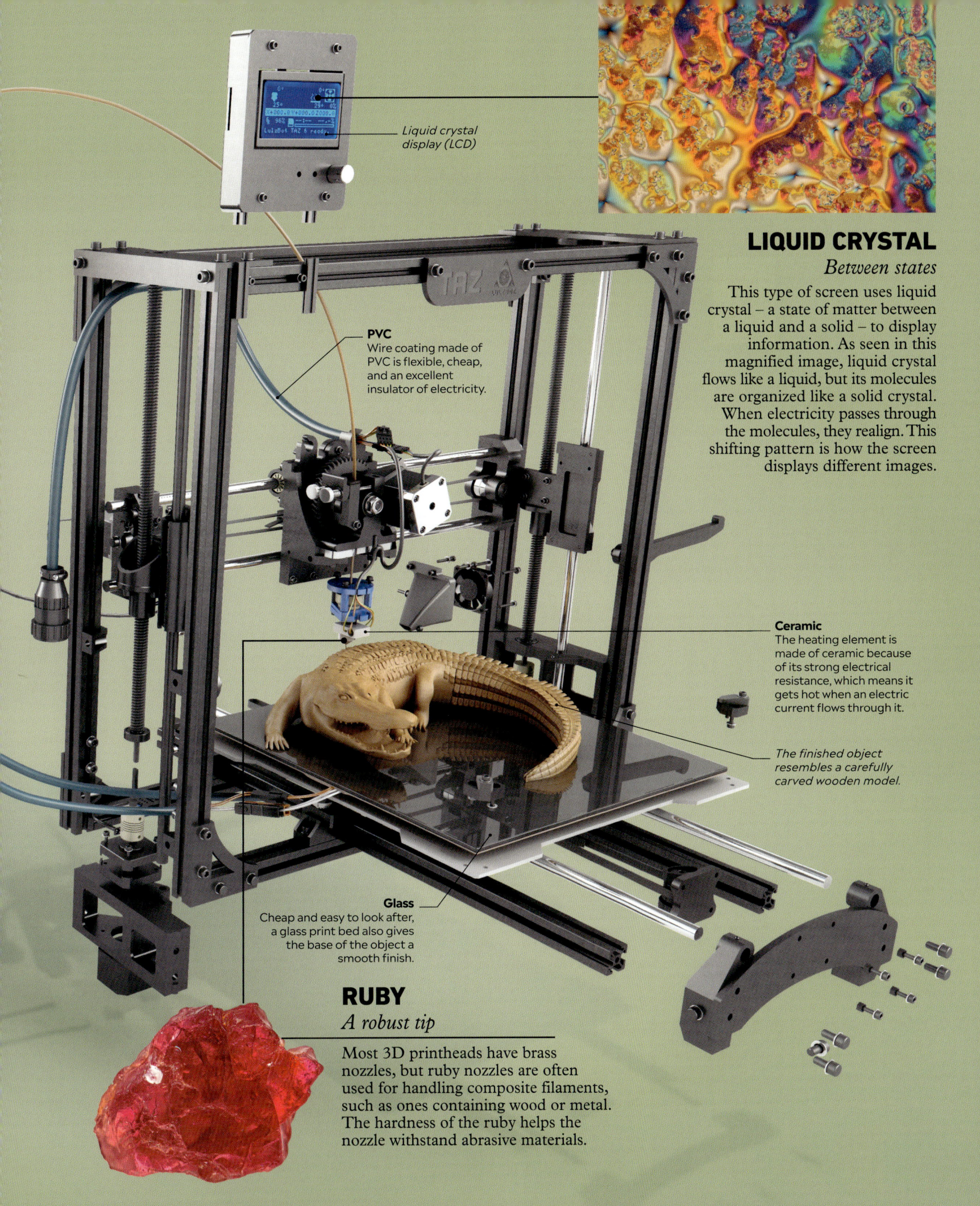

Liquid crystal display (LCD)

PVC
Wire coating made of PVC is flexible, cheap, and an excellent insulator of electricity.

LIQUID CRYSTAL
Between states
This type of screen uses liquid crystal – a state of matter between a liquid and a solid – to display information. As seen in this magnified image, liquid crystal flows like a liquid, but its molecules are organized like a solid crystal. When electricity passes through the molecules, they realign. This shifting pattern is how the screen displays different images.

Ceramic
The heating element is made of ceramic because of its strong electrical resistance, which means it gets hot when an electric current flows through it.

The finished object resembles a carefully carved wooden model.

Glass
Cheap and easy to look after, a glass print bed also gives the base of the object a smooth finish.

RUBY
A robust tip
Most 3D printheads have brass nozzles, but ruby nozzles are often used for handling composite filaments, such as ones containing wood or metal. The hardness of the ruby helps the nozzle withstand abrasive materials.

3D-PRINTED STEEL BRIDGE

This 12-m (40-ft) long bridge across the Oudezijds Achterburgwal canal in Amsterdam, Netherlands, is the world's first 3D-printed steel bridge. Robot arms fitted with welding machines spent six months carefully layering 4,500 kg (9,900 lbs) of stainless steel, giving the bridge its unique texture and curved pattern.

OUT AND ABOUT
USING STEEL

Steel is an alloy of iron with carbon and other elements. It has built the modern world, forming the frames of buildings and vehicles, the bodies of household appliances, tools, and much more. Steel is durable and can be reshaped, drilled, and welded easily. The demand for steel is increasing, with 10 times more steel being produced in 2024 than in 1950.

A grid formed of rebar steel rods acts as a strengthening frame inside concrete.

REBAR

MEDIUM-CARBON STEEL TRAIN WHEELS

Train wheels and railway tracks are made from this robust and durable metal.

LOW-CARBON STEEL WOOL LIGHT DISPLAYS

Steel wool is an abrasive that can be burned to make spectacular light photos.

HIGH-CARBON STEEL PLOUGH BLADES

CARBON STEEL
Nearly 90 per cent of all steel produced is an alloy of iron and carbon. Carbon steel is mostly used in construction and transportation.

High-carbon steel blades are strong, durable, and don't deform easily when pushing heavy loads.

THERE ARE MORE THAN 3,500 DIFFERENT TYPES OF STEEL.

HOW IS IT MADE?
Steel is usually made in a blast furnace and a basic oxygen converter. Iron ore, limestone, and coke (a coal-based fuel) are heated in the furnace. Limestone removes impurities from the ore to produce pig iron, which has a high amount of carbon. It is then blasted with oxygen to remove all carbon content and create pure iron. Carbon is slowly re-added to this iron to create steel.

Iron ore

Limestone

Coke

Varying the amount of carbon creates different types of steel.

Blast furnace
Coke reacts with hot air in the presence of limestone to produce pig iron from iron ore.

Basic oxygen converter
Oxygen is blown through the pig iron to first remove all carbon, before carbon is slowly added back to create steel.

Steel
Molten steel is rolled into rods and sheets, or cast into girders or other shapes.

OUT AND ABOUT 129

TOOL STEEL JACKHAMMER BIT

BUILDING PANELS

The Walt Disney Concert Hall in Los Angeles, US, is covered in stainless steel panels.

Layers of different steels are heated and then hammered together to create these patterned knives.

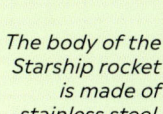
MODERN DAMASCUS STEEL KNIFE

ROCKET BODY

The body of the Starship rocket is made of stainless steel.

STAINLESS STEEL
The addition of up to 18 per cent chromium and up to 8 per cent nickel makes this alloy strong, long-lasting, corrosion-resistant, shiny, and easy-to-clean.

VEHICLE CHASSIS

Advanced high-strength steels are welded together to form a car chassis.

STEEL
Tough iron alloy

Steel is an alloy of iron (the fourth most abundant element in Earth's crust), mixed with 2 per cent or less carbon, and small amounts of other elements. The mixture is melted in a blast furnace to make molten steel, which is then cast into various shapes.

ALLOY STEEL
These steels have other elements added to enhance their strength, hardness, or resistance to corrosion.

Alloy steel rods containing manganese have harder surfaces and are more resistant to strain and shock.

OUT AND ABOUT

ADVANCED CRYSTAL
Heart of the laser

The key to Curiosity's ChemCam laser is a Potassium-Gadolinium Tungstate crystal with small amounts of a rare-earth metal called Neodymium added. The result is a crystal that helps the laser focus more than one million watts of power on a target rock. In 2024, the laser fired its millionth pulse of energy.

Radiation-resistant ties
Made from ethylene-tetrafluoroethylene (ETFE) resin, these zip ties keep cables and pipes in position. The material can withstand 2,000 times more radiation than the regular nylon zip ties used on Earth, as well as extreme temperatures.

The powerful laser can focus on rocks of interest up to 7m (23 ft) away.

Super-strong steel
Vascomax C250 steel is toughened and strengthened with nickel and cobalt. It's used in the actuators that move the robot arm.

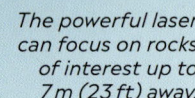

Aluminium
Each of the rover's six wheels is made from a single piece of aluminium and fitted with a grooved tread.

HOW CHEMCAM WORKS

ChemCam fires multiple laser pulses, each lasting just five billionths of a second, at a tiny area of rock. As the laser strikes, the rock turns to plasma and emits different colours of light depending on its elements. This light is gathered by a telescope and analysed by a spectrometer to work out the rock's precise chemical make-up.

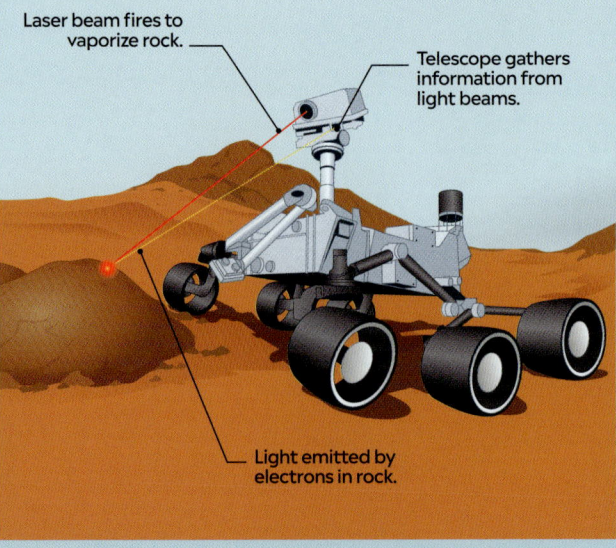

Laser beam fires to vaporize rock.
Telescope gathers information from light beams.
Light emitted by electrons in rock.

MARS ROVER CURIOSITY

NASA's Curiosity rover landed on Mars in 2012 and it's still going strong – proof of its incredible design and the amazing materials used to construct it. The size and weight of a small car, the rover contains ten scientific instruments that examine rocks and soil and investigate whether the planet once harboured life.

OUT AND ABOUT | 131

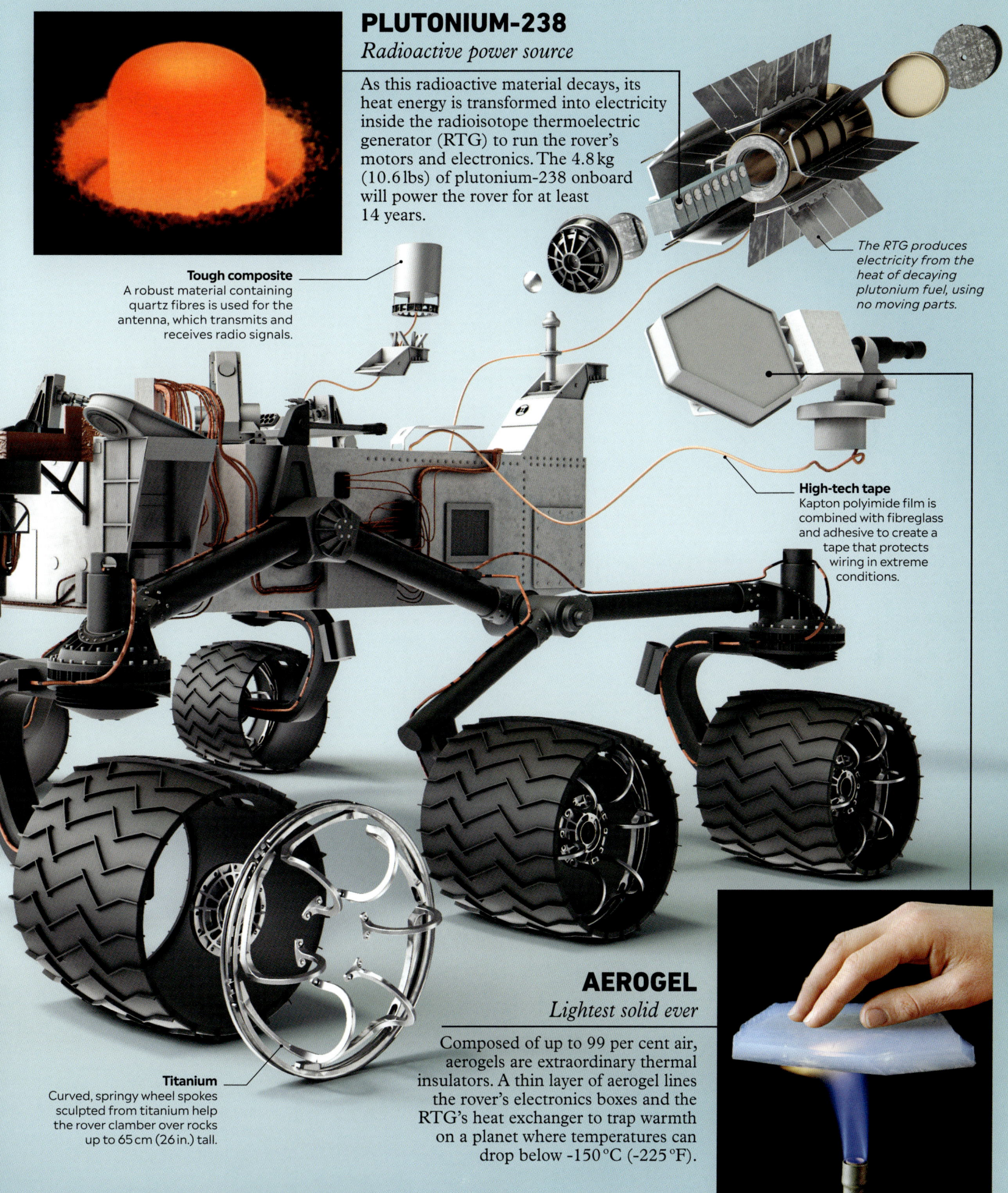

PLUTONIUM-238
Radioactive power source

As this radioactive material decays, its heat energy is transformed into electricity inside the radioisotope thermoelectric generator (RTG) to run the rover's motors and electronics. The 4.8 kg (10.6 lbs) of plutonium-238 onboard will power the rover for at least 14 years.

The RTG produces electricity from the heat of decaying plutonium fuel, using no moving parts.

Tough composite
A robust material containing quartz fibres is used for the antenna, which transmits and receives radio signals.

High-tech tape
Kapton polyimide film is combined with fibreglass and adhesive to create a tape that protects wiring in extreme conditions.

Titanium
Curved, springy wheel spokes sculpted from titanium help the rover clamber over rocks up to 65 cm (26 in.) tall.

AEROGEL
Lightest solid ever

Composed of up to 99 per cent air, aerogels are extraordinary thermal insulators. A thin layer of aerogel lines the rover's electronics boxes and the RTG's heat exchanger to trap warmth on a planet where temperatures can drop below -150 °C (-225 °F).

GOLD
Sight safety

An extremely thin layer of gold – which has extraordinary reflective properties – is applied to the visor. It protects the astronaut's eyes by reflecting ultraviolet and infrared light while allowing visible light to pass through.

GORE-TEX®
Breathable polymer

This waterproof, breathable textile is made from stretched polytetrafluoroethylene. It is blended into the outer layer of the spacesuit (known as the "Ortho-Fabric") where it allows the astronaut's sweat to escape, keeping the wearer dry and comfortable.

NEOPRENE
Insulating rubber

Neoprene coats the nylon used in one of the spacesuit's many layers. It is a synthetic rubber that provides excellent thermal insulation, and forms an airtight seal, keeping oxygen from leaking out.

The Extravehicular Visor Assembly (EVVA) has an extra protective visor that shields the pressure bubble.

The vest-like Hard Upper Torso (HUT) is made of rigid fibreglass to withstand changes in pressure.

The Displays and Control Module (DCM) is mounted on the HUT. Letters and numbers are written backwards so they can be read using a mirror.

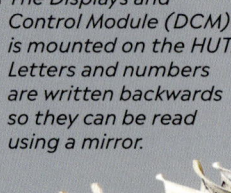

The spacesuit has many outer layers that help keep an astronaut warm in extremely low temperatures.

Nomex®
This durable and flame-resistant fibre is blended into the spacesuit's outer layers.

Kevlar®
This extremely strong fibre is used in the outer layer of the spacesuit to protect astronauts from the high-speed impacts of tiny debris such as micrometeoroids.

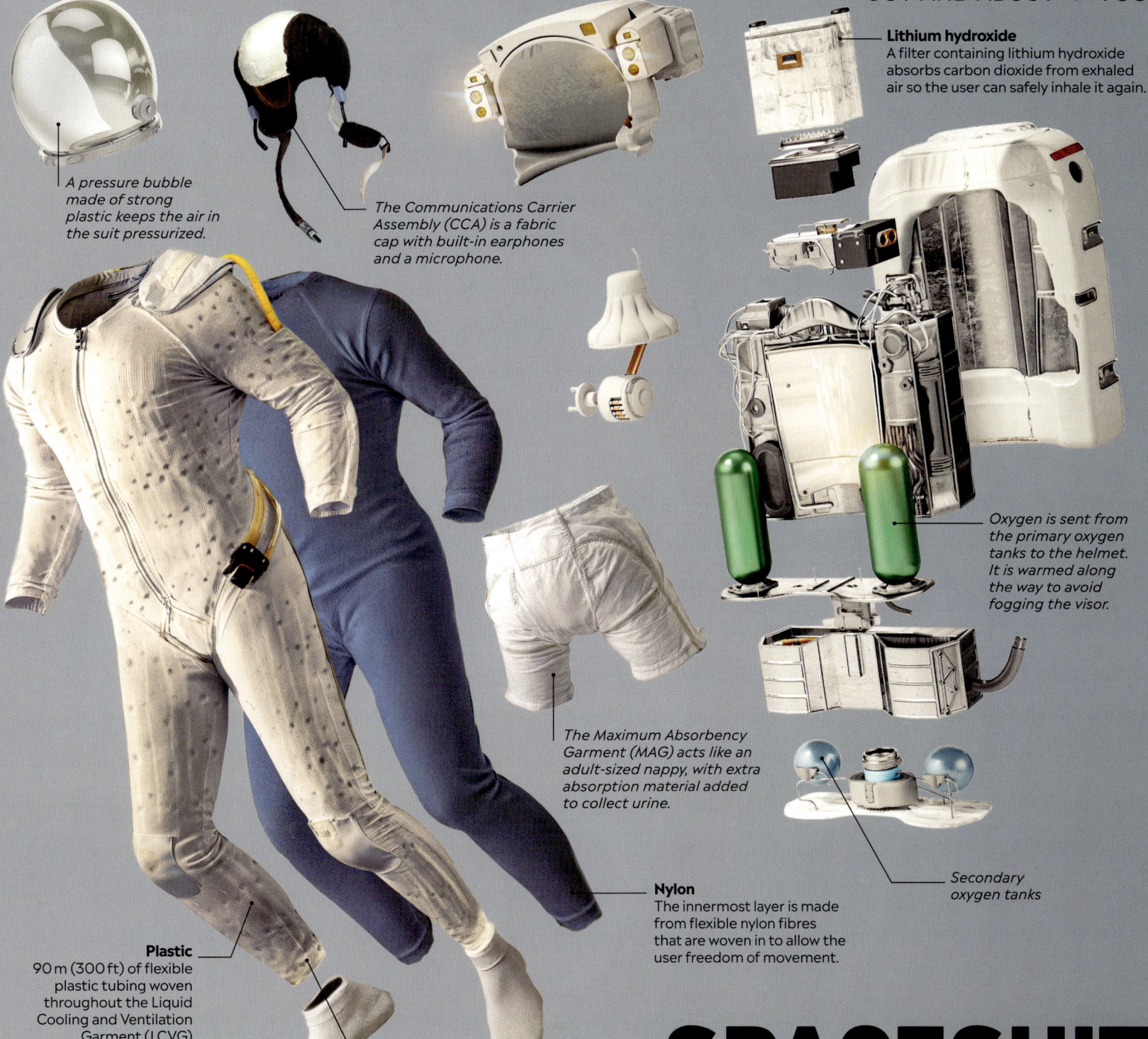

SPACESUIT

Spacesuits protect astronauts against the dangerous radiation, extreme temperatures, and airless vacuum of outer space. The multi-layered spacesuits that astronauts wear outside a spacecraft, such as NASA's Extravehicular Mobility Unit (EMU), are the most complex. They provide all an astronaut needs to be able to perform their tasks in space, from a cooling system and breathable air to an in-built nappy.

A TYPICAL SPACESUIT HAS 14 DIFFERENT LAYERS.

A pressure bubble made of strong plastic keeps the air in the suit pressurized.

The Communications Carrier Assembly (CCA) is a fabric cap with built-in earphones and a microphone.

Lithium hydroxide — A filter containing lithium hydroxide absorbs carbon dioxide from exhaled air so the user can safely inhale it again.

Oxygen is sent from the primary oxygen tanks to the helmet. It is warmed along the way to avoid fogging the visor.

The Maximum Absorbency Garment (MAG) acts like an adult-sized nappy, with extra absorption material added to collect urine.

Secondary oxygen tanks

Nylon — The innermost layer is made from flexible nylon fibres that are woven in to allow the user freedom of movement.

Spandex — Worn inside the spacesuit, the Liquid Cooling and Ventilation Garment (LCVG) is made of a stretchy fabric called spandex.

Plastic — 90 m (300 ft) of flexible plastic tubing woven throughout the Liquid Cooling and Ventilation Garment (LCVG) circulates cold water, keeping the wearer at a comfortable temperature.

OUT AND ABOUT

VERY THIN GOLD LEAF IS SEE-THROUGH.

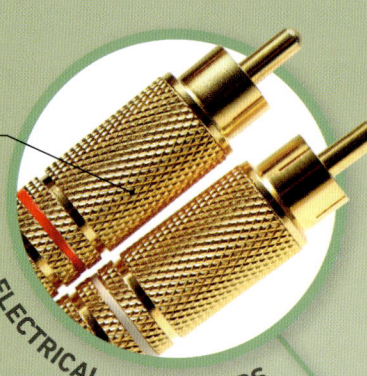

Plugs are gold-plated to enhance the conductivity of audio and visual signals in electronics.

ELECTRICAL CONNECTORS

JAMES WEBB SPACE TELESCOPE

The telescope's mirror is plated with a layer of gold 10,000 times thinner than human hair.

COINAGE
The world's first gold coins were made in the kingdom of Lydia (present-day Turkey) over 2,500 years ago. Gold is still used to mint high-value coins that people purchase as an investment.

GOLD COINS

ASTRONAUT'S HELMET

GOLD PLATING
Applying a very thin layer of expensive gold to cheaper materials is used to make affordable jewellery, and even homewares such as taps and cutlery. Gold plating is also used in space to reflect infrared radiation.

Gold is alloyed with copper, tin, silver, or palladium then moulded into crowns or fillings.

DENTAL GOLD

Solid gold bars are called bullion.

GOLD BULLION

CIRCUIT BOARD

Gold alloy circuit board connectors enable electric signals to flow between circuits.

Gold alloys can also be moulded into bars, just like pure gold.

GOLD ALLOYS
Gold is mixed with other metals to form different alloys. As gold is an excellent conductor of electricity, gold alloys are used in electronics. Another alloy of gold called dental gold is used in repairing teeth.

USING GOLD

Rare and desirable, this dense, soft, and gleaming metal has been used as a marker of wealth for millennia. Gold is malleable and ductile, meaning it can be beaten into thin sheets or shaped into fine wires. It doesn't corrode or react with many chemicals, making it a valuable metal for engineering.

JEWELLERY

Gold has been a symbol of high social status for thousands of years. The ancient Egyptians were among the earliest people to use gold in jewellery and decorations. Pharaoh Tutankhamun's funerary mask (left) from around 1300 BCE is made of alloys of gold.

Gold leaf embedded in the glass windows of the Royal Bank Plaza building in Toronto, Canada, helps reflect heat.

Gold leaf is brushed onto a wooden chair by a craftsperson.

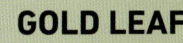

GILDING FURNITURE

CLIMATE-CONTROLLED GLASS

GOLD LEAF

Gold that has been beaten into extremely thin sheets is called gold leaf. It is applied to objects in a process called gilding. Gold leaf can be a mere 25 micrometres (0.001 in) thick.

PURE GOLD
Precious metal

Gold is found as nuggets and grains underground and in river and stream beds. More than a fifth of all the new gold mined each year comes from South Africa. Gold's purity is measured in carats with the purest described as 24 carat.

NANOPARTICLES

Nanoscopic particles of gold called nanoparticles help speed up chemical reactions. They can be added to medicines used to treat arthritis, helping reduce swelling and pain.

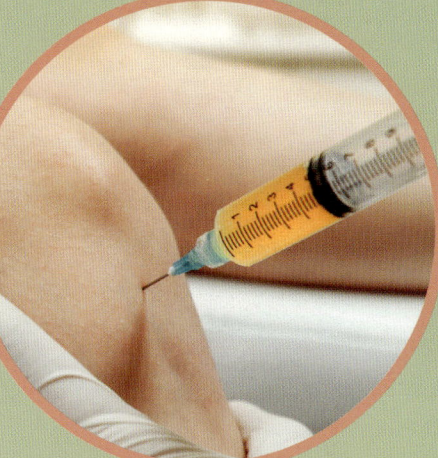

REFERENCE

METALS AND ALLOYS

Humans have been using metals and their alloys for thousands of years. Metals have many useful properties: they are excellent conductors of heat and electricity, are generally hard, resilient materials and can be moulded and hammered into different shapes.

IRON, NICKEL, AND COBALT ARE THE ONLY PURE METALS THAT ARE MAGNETIC.

WHAT IS A METAL?

If you could zoom into a piece of metal you would see it's made up of particles arranged in a regular, repeating pattern. This organized structure is key to many of the typical properties of metals.

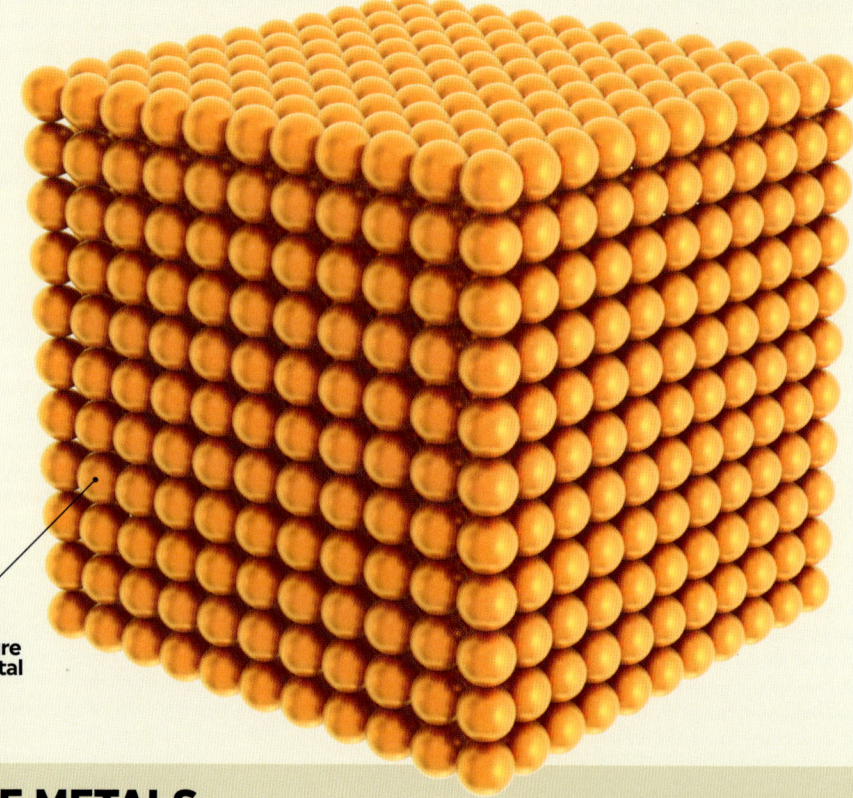

Metals are made up of densely packed particles in a repeating pattern.

Structure of a metal

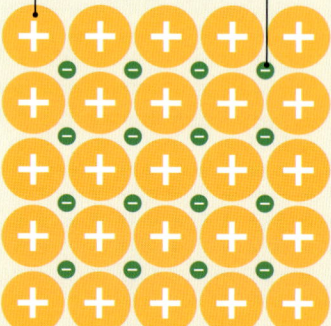

Fixed, positively charged metal ions

Moving, negatively charged electrons

Bonding in metals
Metals are made up of positively charged particles (metal ions) surrounded by freely moving electrons.

PROPERTIES OF METALS

Ductility
Metals, including copper, are ductile, meaning they can be pulled into thin wires without breaking.

Malleability
Metals are malleable. Gold, like other metals, can be bent and moulded into different shapes.

High melting point
Most metals, including iron, have high melting points – it takes lots of energy to disrupt their structure.

Conductors of sound
Metals are sonorous, which means that, like these brass bells, they make a ringing sound when hit.

REFERENCE 139

WHAT IS AN ALLOY?

An alloy is a mixture, either of different metals or of at least one metal and a non-metal. Alloys often have desirable properties. For example, steel contains iron and carbon (and sometimes other metals), and it is harder, stiffer, and stronger than pure iron.

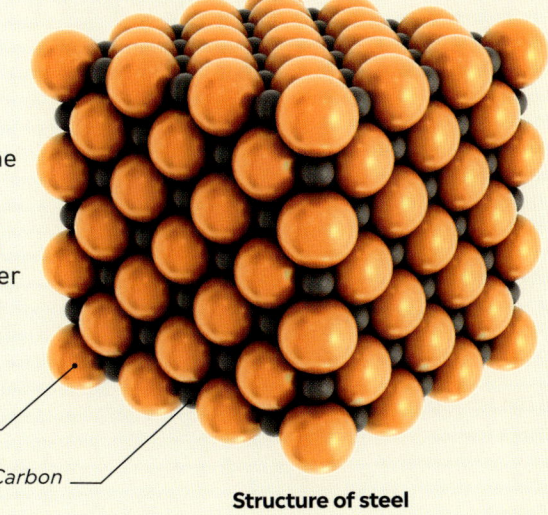

Iron
Carbon
Structure of steel

WHY DO METALS CORRODE?

Corrosion occurs when metals react with one or more substances in the environment. Copper turns brown-black in contact with oxygen, and blue-green when it reacts with carbon dioxide, water and sulphur compounds. Rust is a specific type of corrosion that affects iron and iron alloys when they meet oxygen and water.

Blue-green colour on the copper surface of the Statue of Liberty

Rusty steel hull of a ship

Brown-black colour on the surface of copper-plated coins

HOW DO WE PREVENT CORROSION?

There are different ways to stop corrosion. Paint and plastic coatings stop substances reaching the metal, as does oil. Coating the metal with a more reactive metal – for example, coating iron with zinc – works because the more reactive metal corrodes instead.

Paint or plastic forms a coating

Oil coats and lubricates

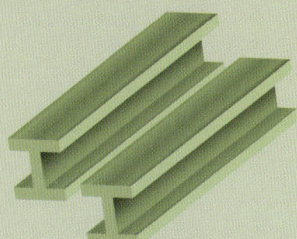
Iron girder coated with the more reactive zinc

APPLICATIONS OF METALS AND ALLOYS

Metals and their alloys are used to make many familiar objects. Some of these are modern inventions while others are much older – 8,000-year-old copper beads have been found in Iraq!

Brass musical instruments
Brass (an alloy of copper and zinc) is used to make the delicate, yet hardwearing twists and turns in musical instruments such as the French horn.

Gold coins and jewellery
Gold stays shiny because it does not react easily. It has been used to make jewellery and coins for thousands of years.

Aluminium alloys in aircraft
Aluminium alloys are light and strong, which makes them the ideal choice for aircraft bodies and parts.

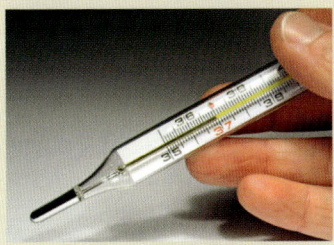

Gallium in thermometers
Gallium has replaced mercury in thermometers because it is less toxic than mercury and is a liquid above 30 °C (86 °F).

Stainless steel utensils
Stainless steel contains iron mixed with carbon, chromium, nickel, and sometimes other metals. It is hard and rustproof, making it useful in the kitchen.

Solder
Solder is an alloy that usually contains tin along with other metals. It is used to connect electrical components.

CARBON MATERIALS

Carbon is well-known for its ability to combine with other elements, but its pure forms are interesting, too. They are very different – diamond is hard and transparent, graphite is soft and opaque, and fullerenes and graphene have their own unique properties.

ALL LIVING THINGS CONTAIN CARBON.

KINDS OF CARBON

People have used the different forms of carbon throughout history. Diamonds have been in use for more than 2,000 years, while graphite was first used for writing in the 1500s. Fullerenes were only discovered in the 1980s.

Graphene powder contains tiny sheets of carbon.

Graphene powder

Diamond

Graphite

Graphite is used in pencils because it is soft enough to leave a mark on paper when writing or drawing.

Soft graphite in pencil

USES OF CARBON

Diamond-coated drill bit
Diamond is used in some drills because it is the hardest naturally occurring substance on Earth.

Graphite grease
The layers in graphite slide over each other, making it an excellent, oil-free lubricant.

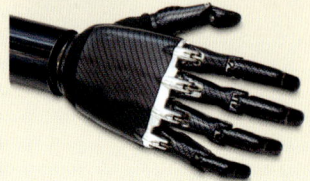

Carbon fibre prosthetic
Carbon fibres are very thin and strong. They can be used to make strong, lightweight prosthetic arms that resist wear and tear.

CARBON STRUCTURES

Carbon has different physical forms based on the number of bonds formed by its atoms. Carbon atoms form four bonds with each other in diamonds, but only three bonds with one another in graphite.

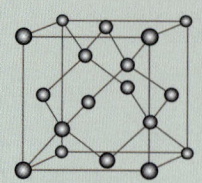

Diamond
Diamond's rigid, crystalline structure makes it very hard.

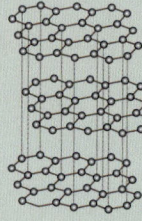

Graphite
The layers in graphite are weakly attracted, so can easily slide over each other.

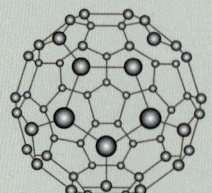

Fullerene
Fullerenes are carbon molecules in the shape of spheres or tubes.

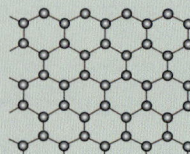

Graphene
Graphene is made up of a single layer of carbon atoms in a hexagonal grid.

NOBLE GASES

The elements called noble gases sit on the far right of the periodic table. They are called "noble" as they tend not to react with other substances. They are gaseous at room temperature and pressure, and are not flammable.

NICE NOBLES

They might be colourless under ordinary circumstances, but noble gases have a very interesting property – they glow different colours when electricity passes through them.

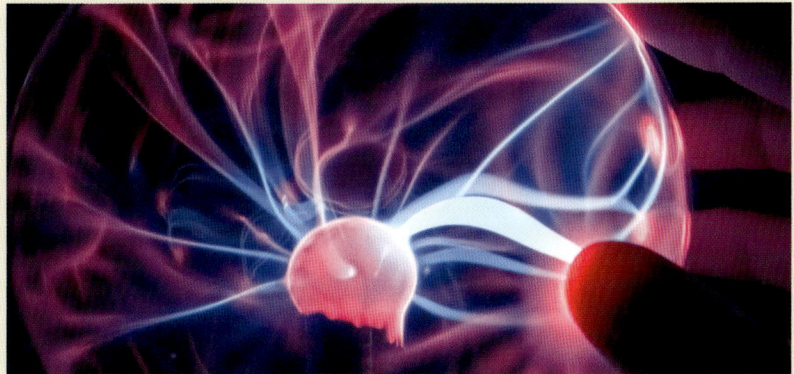

Plasma ball
A plasma ball is filled with a mixture of noble gases. Passing electricity through the ball produces colourful light beams as each gas glows a different colour.

Helium is the lightest of the noble gases.

Noble gases on the periodic table
In the periodic table, elements in the same group have similar properties. Noble gases, which do not react easily, sit together in group 18 of the table.

NOBLE GASES HAVE NO COLOUR, TASTE, OR SMELL.

USES OF NOBLE GASES

The useful properties of noble gases lead to many important applications in everyday life.

Helium balloons
Both helium and hydrogen are lighter than air, but helium doesn't burn, making it safer for inflating balloons and blimps.

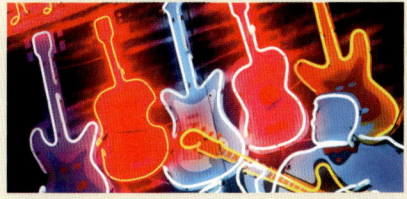

Neon signs
Passing electricity through neon causes it to glow orange-red. Other substances can be added to change the glow's colour.

Argon in food packaging
Non-reactive argon forms a barrier around food that protects it from oxygen, so food stays fresh longer.

Krypton light bulbs
Krypton is used in some light bulbs as it produces a very bright, white light.

Xenon in car headlights
Bulbs containing xenon have been used in car headlights for their blue-white light and longer lifespan.

Radioactive radon
Radon is radioactive and is found underground. By tracking radon it is possible to identify groundwater sources.

GLASS, CERAMICS, AND CONCRETE

> CONCRETE IS THE SECOND-MOST USED SUBSTANCE IN THE WORLD AFTER WATER.

Humans have been building structures for more than 10,000 years. We have developed all sorts of materials for this purpose – including bricks, ceramics, cement, concrete, and glass. Many of them have changed little between the distant past and the present day in terms of their composition.

ALL AROUND THE HOUSE

Exactly which materials are used to build a house depends on the cost, weather conditions, and local culture. It is vital to consider the environment inside and outside the building. A house has to be insulated from outside heat or cold, for example, to maintain a comfortable temperature inside the building.

Bricks, made by firing clay at high temperatures, are used to construct walls.

Hard, transparent glass is the ideal material for windows, which have to let light in but keep cold air out.

Roof tiles can be made of ceramic or other materials such as slate or metal.

Plaster, or "render", is used to give a smooth or decorative finish to walls.

BUILDING WITH GLASS

Glass is a hard and durable building material that is mostly made of silica (a compound of silicon and oxygen commonly found in sand). It is produced by rapidly cooling a hot, liquid mixture, and it is easy to shape into a variety of objects in its liquid state. As glass is cooled quickly its particles become fixed in a disordered manner. This makes it an "amorphous" solid, meaning there is no order to the arrangement of its particles. This differs from other silica-based materials, such as the crystal, quartz, which have well-ordered particle structures.

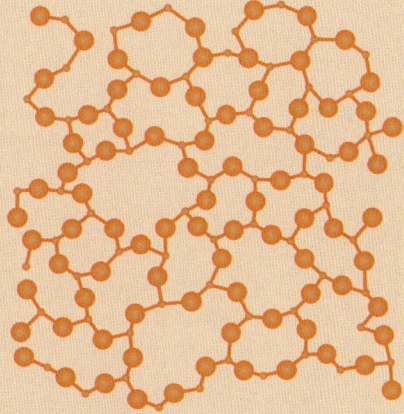

Glass (amorphous solid)
The structure of glass is disorderly, like a liquid, but its particles stay bonded in fixed positions.

Quartz crystal (solid)
Here, particles are arranged in a rigid, orderly pattern. Crystals can be transparent or opaque.

SUPER CERAMICS

Clay is a natural material. It is mouldable when wet, but when heated to high temperatures (fired), it forms a hard ceramic that is resistant to heat and corrosion. Such ceramics are porous, but when painted with glassy substances called glazes and re-fired, they become water-resistant.

Glazed ceramics
Glazes are substances painted onto fired ceramic, which is then re-fired. They produce a glassy coating which makes the ceramic wear- and water-resistant. Glazed ceramics are used to make plates and bowls, as well as wall and floor tiles.

Bricks
Traditionally, single bricks are made from fired clay. Bricks are then joined together using mortar (usually a mixture of sand, cement, and water) to make the walls of structures.

Advanced ceramics
Ceramics can withstand extremely high temperatures. Ultra-high-temperature ceramics (UHTCs) used in rocket thrusters can be heated to 2,000°C (3,600°F) and stay solid!

CEMENT AND CONCRETE

Cement and concrete have been used for construction for thousands of years – the earliest recordings of concrete structures date back to 6,500 BCE! Cement is made from a sedimentary rock called limestone and is used as a binding agent for construction materials. Concrete is a composite material containing small stones (aggregate) mixed with cement.

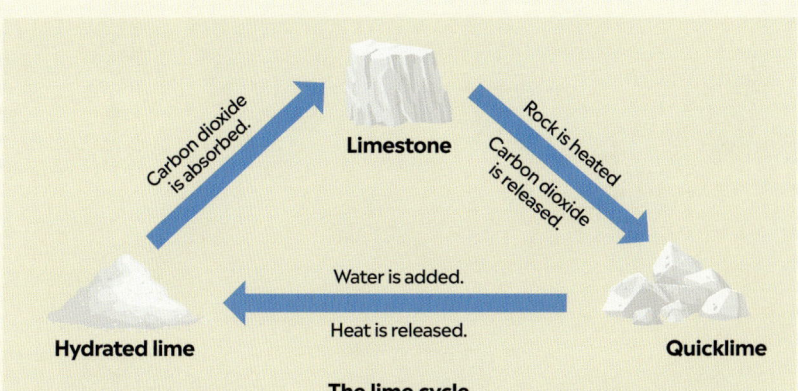

The lime cycle
Limestone is the basis for many essential building materials. When heated it turns into quicklime, which is used to make cement and concrete. Adding water to quicklime creates hydrated lime, which is used in mortar. Hydrated lime turns back into limestone when exposed to carbon dioxide.

Concrete
Freshly prepared concrete is a paste made from cement, water, and small stones. When left to dry, the cement hardens around the stones, creating a strong, rocklike material.

NATURAL MATERIALS

Many of the materials we use most often are found in nature rather than produced in a factory or laboratory. To prepare these materials for use it is often necessary to process them by weaving, dyeing, or cutting, but we still think of them as natural materials.

HUMANS HAVE BUILT THINGS USING WOOD FOR ABOUT 300,000 YEARS.

WOOD

Wood is a very useful material – it is strong and easy to cut into different shapes. There are many types of wood, from lightweight balsa to dense, resilient mahogany and oak. If they are given the right pressure treatment and paint or varnish, wooden items can be made to last for many years.

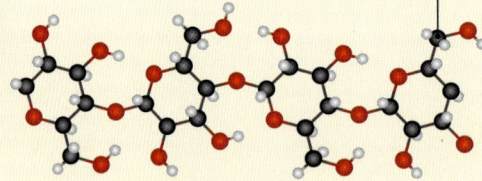

Cellulose, the most abundant natural polymer on Earth, makes up about 50 per cent of all wood.

Cellulose
This substance supports the structure of plant cells, helping plants stay upright, and makes wood a stiff, sturdy material.

Wooden furniture
Wood is a popular material for furniture as it is strong, durable, and warm to the touch.

COTTON

Cotton grows in round, fluffy "bolls" around the seeds of cotton plants. After the bolls have been harvested, the fibres are spun into yarn or thread, which can be used to make clothes, sheets, and other textiles. Cotton is one of the most widely used fabrics in the world.

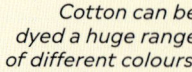

Cotton can be dyed a huge range of different colours.

Cotton "bolls" have a tough outer shell, which surrounds the cotton fibres.

Cotton fabric
Many people like the feel of cotton against their skin as this versatile fabric is soft, breathable, and comfortable.

REFERENCE | 145

RUBBER

A milky white substance called latex, harvested from Pará rubber trees, is treated with sulphur (vulcanization) to create natural rubber. Most synthetic rubber is made from crude oil.

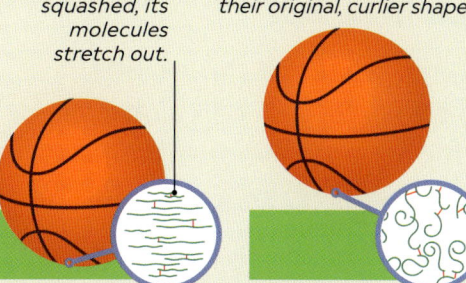

When rubber is squashed, its molecules stretch out.

The molecules then return to their original, curlier shape.

How rubber molecules act
Rubber molecules have lots of folds, which straighten out during impact but return to their normal shape afterwards. This property is called elasticity.

Car tyre
Rubber's elasticity means it can absorb shocks and provide grip – essential for car tyres.

SILK

People in China have processed silk for at least 5,000 years. *Bombyx mori* moths lay their eggs on mulberry leaves, which are then eaten by the larvae (silkworms). These larvae spin a cocoon from a single silk thread, which can be 300–900 m (1,000–3,000 ft) long.

Silk can be dyed to make colourful fabrics like these ties.

It takes about 7 kg (15 lbs) of cocoons to produce 1 kg (2 lbs) of silk thread.

Silk fabric
Silk is a luxurious fabric known for its smooth texture. Clothes made of silk are lustrous with a soft, slippery feel.

WOOL

As well as from sheep, wool is also made from the hair of other animals such as goats, llamas, and some types of rabbit. The hair is collected, washed, spun into fibres, and dyed. Wool is a polymer like nylon, but moisture can pass more easily through wool fabrics.

Wool "wicks", or pulls, sweat away from the skin, keeping us warm without overheating.

Wool is often made from the fleecy coats of sheep.

Wool fabric
Wool fibres are excellent at retaining heat, making woollen garments, such as sweaters, perfect for chilly weather.

SYNTHETIC POLYMERS

Repeating groups of atoms make up large molecules called polymers. They occur in nature, but can also be made in laboratories and factories. Human-made polymers are called synthetic polymers, and many of them are familiar to us as plastics.

THE FIRST SYNTHETIC POLYMER, BAKELITE, WAS INVENTED IN 1907.

HOW DO POLYMERS FORM?

Monomers are small molecules that can chemically react with each other. Once this reaction is triggered, the monomers join together to form long polymer chains that can have very different, and often very useful, properties.

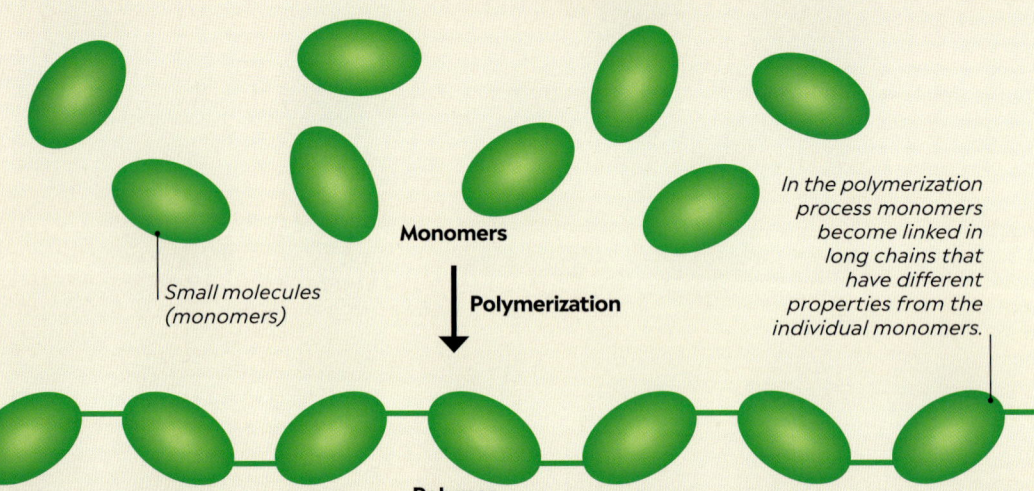

Small molecules (monomers)

Monomers

Polymerization

In the polymerization process monomers become linked in long chains that have different properties from the individual monomers.

Long polymer chain

Polymer

PROPERTIES OF SYNTHETIC POLYMERS

Synthetic polymers are designed to have specific properties, such as transparency and flexibility. Most are lightweight and non-reactive, giving them advantages over natural materials such as metal and wood.

Lightweight and flexible polyethylene is used to make plastic bags.

Hard, transparent polycarbonate can be used to make windows.

Polystyrene is a good insulator – it can be used to keep drinks hot.

Silicone is heat-resistant, inert, and non-stick, making it useful for cooking.

TYPES OF POLYMER

Thermosoftening polymers are made up of molecules with weak bonds between them that can be broken by heat. The molecules of thermosetting polymers are more strongly bonded together, so they are hard and more heat-resistant.

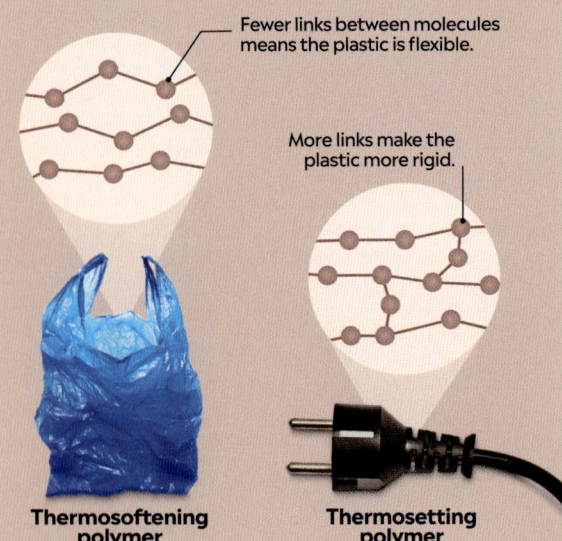

Fewer links between molecules means the plastic is flexible.

More links make the plastic more rigid.

Thermosoftening polymer

Thermosetting polymer

REFERENCE | 147

EXAMPLES OF POLYMERS

NYLON 6,6

There are several different kinds of nylon. The first was made in 1935 and is named nylon 6,6 because its monomers each contain six carbon atoms. It is used to make a range of products, including toothbrush bristles, sportswear, tights, and backpacks.

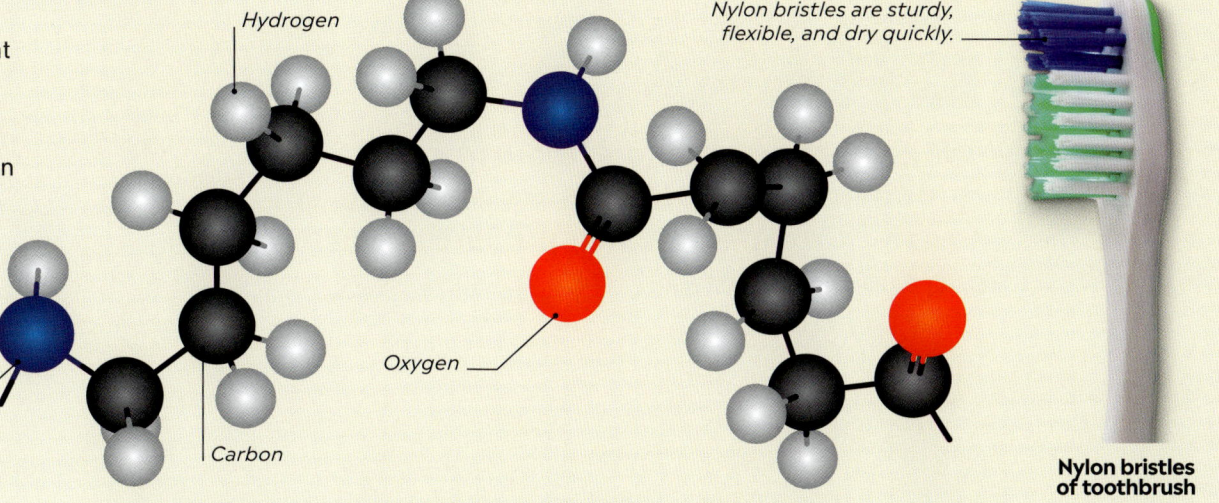

Nylon bristles of toothbrush

Nylon bristles are sturdy, flexible, and dry quickly.

POLYETHYLENE

Ethene monomers contain two carbon atoms, with two hydrogen atoms linked to each carbon. When these monomers join, they form polythene (polyethylene). Different types of polyethylene have different properties. More polyethylene is made than any other plastic.

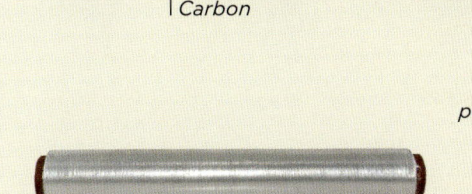

Low-density polyethylene film

Low-density polyethylene (LDPE) is used to make flexible materials, such as plastic wrap.

High-density polyethylene pipe

High-density polyethylene (HDPE) is used to make products that need to be rigid.

POLYVINYL CHLORIDE (PVC)

Millions of tonnes of polyvinyl chloride (PVC) are produced each year. Each of its monomers contain two carbon atoms, with one carbon linked to two hydrogen atoms and the other to one hydrogen and one chlorine atom. Chemicals called plasticizers are often added to PVC to make it softer and more flexible. This plastic is used to make flooring, vinyl records, and "fake leather" bags and shoes.

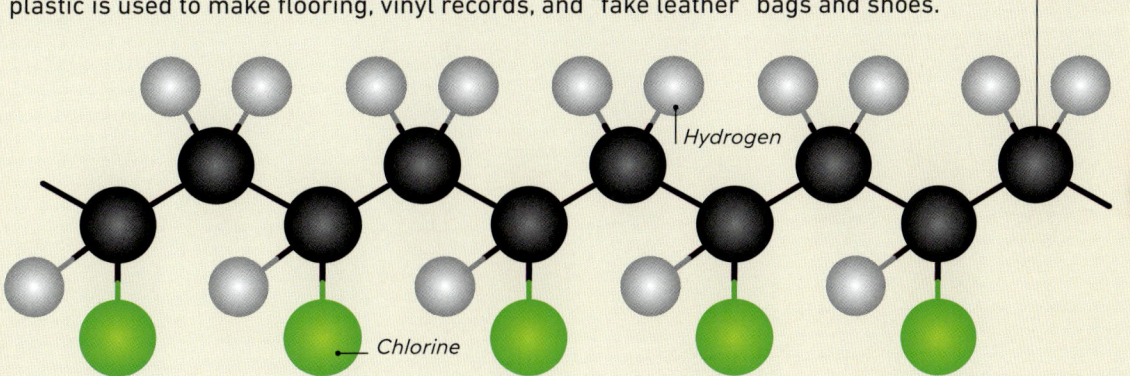

PVC wire insulation

PVC is used to make insulation for cables and wires because it is flexible and does not conduct electricity.

COMPOSITE MATERIALS

Composite materials are made from two or more materials that have different properties. The materials are combined to make something new that combines their properties, such as being both strong and very light.

> **ADDING THIN GLASS OR PLASTIC FIBRES CAN MAKE TRANSLUCENT CONCRETE.**

FIBREGLASS

Fibreglass is a cheap, strong, lightweight, and water-resistant composite material made from glass and plastic. To make it, heated glass is drawn into fine, strong fibres, which are embedded in plastic. Fibreglass is used to make boats, pipes, and even swimming pools.

Glass fibres embedded in plastic sheeting

MAKING COMPOSITES

Two common kinds of composite, fibre- and particle-reinforced composites, contain two key elements: a binding agent, or matrix, to bind together different substances and reinforcement, or filler. Concrete is an example of a particle-reinforced composite, while carbon fibres are used to make fibre-reinforced composites. Composite laminates are made by fusing layers of different material, such as wood or graphite.

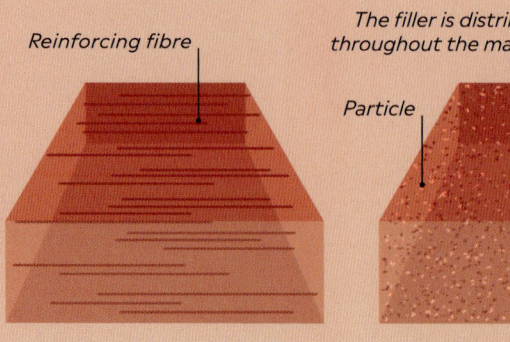

Reinforcing fibre

Fibre-reinforced composite

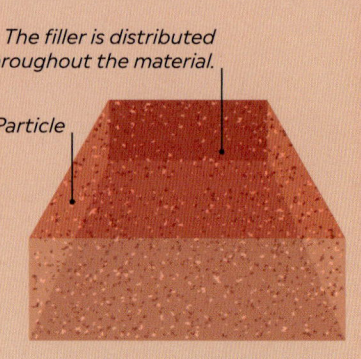

The filler is distributed throughout the material.
Particle

Particle-reinforced composite

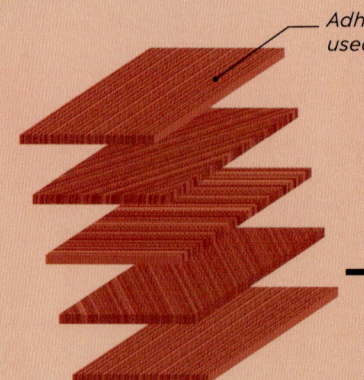

Adhesives such as resin may be used to bind the layers together.

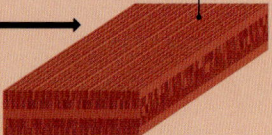

The final laminate is stiffer and stronger than a "pure" material.

Composite laminates

REFERENCE | 149

ANCIENT COMPOSITES

Humans have been making composite materials for thousands of years. Wattle and daub buildings – where a wooden lattice is covered with a sticky mixture of wet soil, clay, and sand or straw – were being built 6,000 years ago. Cob mud bricks are also thousands of years old.

Wattle and daub hut

Cob mud bricks

Ancient Egyptians used a material similar to papier-mâché (made from layers of papyrus or linen covered with plaster) to make coffins.

Egyptian coffin

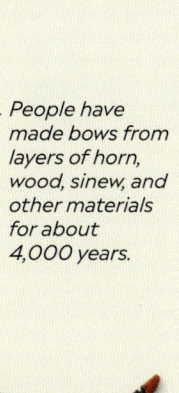

People have made bows from layers of horn, wood, sinew, and other materials for about 4,000 years.

Composite bow

TYPES OF COMPOSITE MATERIAL

Composite materials are all around us – composite fabrics are used to make fire-resistant and waterproof clothing, reinforced plastics are common in sports equipment, and a lot of modern furniture is made of engineered wood.

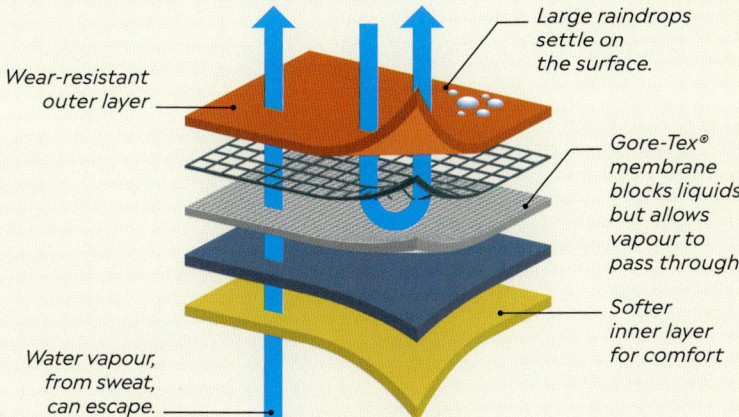

Wear-resistant outer layer
Large raindrops settle on the surface.
Gore-Tex® membrane blocks liquids, but allows vapour to pass through.
Softer inner layer for comfort
Water vapour, from sweat, can escape.

Fabric composites
Composite fabrics are enhanced textiles used to make durable, protective clothing. For example, Gore-Tex® clothes (above) are waterproof but breathable.

Carbon fibres embedded in a ceramic matrix.

Ceramic matrix composites
Lightweight ceramic matrix composites (CMCs) can withstand high temperatures, making them useful in aviation and rocketry.

Reinforced plastics
Fibre-reinforced plastics are strong and lightweight. Sports equipment is often reinforced with carbon fibre.

Composite wood
Composite wood, such as plywood, is made by binding different layers of wood together, usually with adhesives (glues).

RECYCLING AND SUSTAINABILITY

Making any object requires raw materials and energy, but planet Earth has a limited supply of natural resources such as metals and fossil fuels. Recycling reuses our limited resources and reduces waste, while sustainable living helps us reduce our impact on the planet.

RECYCLING AND REUSING

Recycling saves resources by using materials that have fulfilled their original use. Recycling requires energy, but less than the energy needed to make new things, and some materials can be reused without needing to be recycled.

METAL
Most metals can be recycled endlessly. Recycling one tonne of aluminium produces up to nine tonnes less carbon dioxide than the process of extracting the metal from ore.

Crushed aluminium cans

GLASS
Most glass items, such as bottles, jars, and window glass, are reusable and recyclable. Glass collected for recycling is sorted by colour, crushed into smaller pieces, and melted to make new objects.

Glass waste

PLASTIC
There are many types of plastic, and some of them can be recycled. However, each type needs to be separated from the others, which makes recycling plastic a difficult and costly process.

Used plastic bottles

WOOD
Pieces of good-quality wood can be recovered from discarded material and used to make household items. Lower-quality wood is broken down to make animal bedding or woodchip pellets.

Wood shredder producing wood chips

TEXTILES
Discarded fabrics and textile waste must be sorted by material and colour before they can be shredded to make fibres. These fibres are spun into yarns and then woven into new fabric.

Textile waste

CONCRETE
Old concrete can't be recycled, but it can be crushed into small particles to make building material. Crushed concrete is used as aggregate and to construct roads in some countries.

Concrete waste at a landfill

REFERENCE | 151

SUSTAINABLE LIVING

The limited resources of the planet can be preserved for future generations if they are used sustainably. This means using fewer new raw materials and less energy during production, along with recycling and reusing materials when possible. We can also ensure sustainable production and use by making energy-efficient products that last longer, reducing waste.

Energy is needed to get raw materials.

Manufacturing

Factories can utilize recycled materials to make new products to lower energy and resource use.

Recycling

Recycling takes some energy, but not as much as making "new" products.

Some things can't be recycled, but these should be the exception, not the rule.

Making energy-efficient products that can be repaired, reused, or recycled saves resources.

Consumption and use

HARD-TO-RECYCLE MATERIALS

Some materials cannot be recycled easily and have to be reused or disposed of. Composite materials, such as foil-lined packaging, are often difficult to recycle because they are made up of different types of material that can be difficult to separate.

DISPOSAL

Material that cannot be reused or recycled is disposed of as waste. Food and garden waste can be composted. Some types of waste, such as plastics, can be burned, but doing so releases harmful gases. A lot of waste is also sent to landfill sites as a last resort, where there is a risk it may continue to pollute.

Foil-lined packaging

Composting facility

GLOSSARY

3D PRINTER FILAMENT
Continuous and slender plastic or composite thread, often stored on reels, which is heated and fused in a 3D printhead. The printer then deposits a small amount of plastic as it builds up a printed object layer by layer.

AGGREGATE
A collection of different hard materials, including stones, stone chips, sand, and gravel, used to add bulk in mixtures in the construction industry.

ALLOY
A material made by combining two or more elements. Most alloys are made with metals, but some contain non-metals. The non-metal carbon, for example, is an important ingredient in steel.

ANODE
One of the two electrodes in a battery. An anode is an electrical conductor through which electrons can move. When a battery is in use, electrons flow from the anode to the cathode. When the battery is charging, the opposite happens and electrons flow from the cathode to the anode.

ANTENNA
A device that converts electrical signals into radio waves, or receives radio waves and converts them into electrical signals. Antennae are found in everything from spacecraft to smartwatches and phones.

ATOM
The building block for all matter. Anything that has mass and occupies space consists of atoms. Each atom has a nucleus made up of smaller particles called protons, neutrons, and electrons.

CAST
The process of pouring liquids into a mould, which then set to form a solid, finished object.

CATALYST
A substance that changes the rate of a chemical reaction without being used up or changed itself. Catalysts are used in the chemicals industry to speed up reactions.

CATHODE
One of the two electrodes in a battery. See anode, above, for further explanation.

CERAMIC
Materials that are neither metals nor organic solids and that permanently harden when heated. Brick, porcelain, and earthenware are all ceramics.

CHASSIS
The frame of a motor vehicle, computer or another device, which supports and bears the weight or load of the rest of the machine.

COMPOSITE
A material made of two or more different materials each with differing physical and chemical properties. Concrete reinforced with steel is one commonly used composite; fibreglass is another.

COMPOUND
A material or substance made of two or more chemical elements with its atoms bonded together. The elements can only be separated from each other by chemical reactions.

COOLANT
A substance, most commonly a liquid – although air is also used – which carries away heat to cool machinery or a process down.

CORROSION
The deterioration and wearing away of a metal or metal alloy due to chemical reactions with its environment. The rusting of steel and iron is a common example of corrosion.

ELECTROLYTE
A liquid that conducts electricity through the movement of its ions.

ELECTRON
An extremely small particle found in atoms, outside of their nucleus, which has a negative electrical charge. The atoms of different elements have differing numbers of electrons.

ELEMENT
An element is made of just one type of atom and all known elements are listed on the periodic table.

EMISSIONS
Gases and particles that are sent up into the atmosphere. It is most commonly used to describe substances sent into the atmosphere by human activities such as burning fossil fuels.

EVAPORATION
The change of state of a liquid that turns into a gas, such as liquid water evaporating into water vapour. The opposite change of state – a gas changing into a liquid – is called condensation.

FABRIC
Any cloth or cloth-like material made by knitting, weaving, or interlacing fibres in other ways.

FIBRE
Thread-like parts of plants, the fur or fleece of animals, or human-made materials such as polyester or nylon that can be woven or joined together in some way to make cloth or rope.

GALVANIZED
When a base metal is coated or plated with a thin layer of zinc to protect the base metal from its surroundings. Galvanizing most commonly prevents rusting of iron and steel.

GAS
A state of matter where the substance has no fixed shape or volume. The atoms and molecules in a gas move constantly and are far apart meaning gases can be compressed.

GYPSUM
A soft white or white-grey mineral widely used in making plaster of Paris as well as cement, plasterboard, and plaster for the walls of buildings. Gypsum is also used as a filler in some types of paper.

INSULATOR
Any material which stops or inhibits the flow of either electricity or heat. Good thermal insulators are used to keep heat in homes and cold air inside refrigerators, increasing energy efficiency.

ION
An atom that has an electric charge because it has either lost electrons or gained additional electrons. An ion with a positive charge is called a cation. One with a negative charge is known as an anion.

KILN
A form of oven used to dry out, bake or harden certain materials, especially clays and other ceramics. Specialist kilns are also used to remove the high moisture content of freshly cut down trees.

LAMINATE
To manufacture a material made up of a number of layers. Lamination may add strength to the finished material, improve its appearance or make it waterproof depending on the materials used.

LIME
A group of calcium oxides and calcium hydroxides derived from limestone rock. They are widely used in construction in mortars, in the production of cement, and in steelmaking to remove impurities from the metal.

GLOSSARY

LIQUID
A state of matter where the substance has a fixed volume but no fixed shape. It can flow and take the shape of a container but cannot be easily compressed.

LUBRICANT
A substance used to reduce the rubbing force of friction between two different objects in contact. Lubricants such as oils, waxes and grease can help reduce the heat and wear created by friction.

MALLEABLE
A property of materials. A malleable metal, for example, is a metal that can be pressed, beaten or rolled into thin sheets without breaking.

MATRIX
A component of a composite material that binds the other component, the reinforcement, together.

MICROWAVE
A type of electromagnetic wave with wavelengths shorter than radio waves but longer than infrared waves. Microwaves are used in communications, sensors, and in ovens to heat and cook food.

MINERAL
A natural, inorganic substance. Most rocks are made of minerals.

MOLECULE
A group of two or more atoms which are chemically bonded together. The atoms can be the same or different chemical elements. A water molecule, for example, is made of one oxygen and two hydrogen atoms.

MOULD
Some form of specially sculpted container in which a material is poured or injected and takes the shape of the inside of the mould. Plastics, metals, glass, and some ceramic materials can all be moulded.

NANOSCOPIC
Something so small it is measured in nanometres. One nanometre is one billionth of a metre. This page is 235 million nanometres wide.

OLED
Short for Organic Light-Emitting Diode, these are electronic devices made of a sandwich of thin films. OLEDs give off light and are used in some high-resolution computer and TV screens.

ORE
A type of mineral that contains useful and valuable metals which can be extracted. Much of the world's aluminium, for example, is extracted from bauxite ores.

ORGANIC
A word describing carbon-based materials or substances. Many, like wood and natural rubber, are derived from living things. Others, like plastics, are made in labs or by the chemicals industry.

OVEN
An enclosed space that exposes materials to heat and high temperatures. Ovens are used in food cooking but also in making some metals and types of glass as well as other materials.

OXIDIZATION
The process when a material or substance oxidizes, meaning it reacts and combines with oxygen. Combustion – when fuel burns in air (which contains oxygen) – is an oxidizing reaction, as is the rusting of iron.

PARTICLE
A tiny speck of matter, or a name for the components of an atom (proton, neutron, electron).

PLASMA
A state of matter where energy has caused some of the atoms in a gas to be ripped apart. The resulting plasma is a mixture of electrons, ions, and atoms.

PLASTIC
Any synthetic or semi-synthetic material made from polymers which can be shaped or moulded. Common plastics include PVC, PET, acrylic and polyethylene.

POLYMER
A very long molecule made up of lots of small, repeating molecules known as monomers which are all joined together.

PRESSURE
The amount of force felt when something presses against a surface. It is measured in pascals (Pa), Newtons per square centimetre, bars, or pounds per square inch (PSI).

RADIATION
Energy travelling as electromagnetic particles or waves such as infrared, ultraviolet, or visible light. Some forms of radiation can be harmful to life.

REFINE
To remove impurities from metals or to separate out different fractions of crude oil into separate petroleum products such as gasoline and bitumen.

SMELT
A way of extracting a valuable metal or compound from an ore by heating it in the presence of a reducing agent (e.g. coke in iron smelting).

SOLID
One of the states of matter. Solids can be held, cut and shaped and stay in one place. They do not spread like gases or flow like liquids.

SOLUTION
A mixture containing one or more solutes – substances that can be dissolved in another substance, which is called the solvent.

SOLVENT
A substance that can dissolve other substances.

STATE
Matter can be in one of four forms: solid, liquid, gas, or plasma. The addition or removal of energy can see matter change state, such as when a solid metal is heated, melts and turns into a molten liquid.

SYNTHETIC
Something which does not occur in nature and is made by humans using chemical or other technological processes. Many fabrics, such as polyester, acrylic, and nylon, are synthetic.

TEMPERATURE
A measure of the amount of heat contained in an object or its surroundings. It is measured with a thermometer using one of three common temperature scales: Celsius, Fahrenheit, or Kelvin.

TEXTILE
Any material made of interlacing fibres such as knitted woollen cloth or woven fabrics. It is also used to describe the industry that produces the fibres and yarns used to manufacture fabrics.

THERMAL
Relating to heat. If a material is a good thermal conductor, it allows heat to travel through it easily.

THERMOPLASTIC
A plastic which softens when heated and hardens once cooled without any changes in its chemical properties. Such plastics can be heated and cooled multiple times, making them easy to recycle.

INDEX

Main topics are shown in **bold** page numbers.

A

acids
 acrylic 54
 oleic acid 15
 polylactic acid (PLA) 28, 124
 sulphuric 103
acrylic
 aircraft 116
 paints 54
 pianos 63
 rugs 67
acrylonitrile butadiene styrene (ABS) 46, 89, 112
adhesives 56-57, 72, 101
advanced ceramics 93, 143
advanced crystal 130
aerogel 33, 131
airbags **106-107**
air conditioners 25
aircraft 13, **116-117**, 139
aliphatic polyesters 28
alloys **138-139**
 see also steel
aluminium **12-13**, 139
 in alloys 25, 32, 117
 food packaging 29, 81
 football boots 43
 headphones 11
 microwave ovens 79
 skis 100
 smartphones 23
 spacecraft 130
ammonium phosphate and sulphate 74
animal-derived materials 67, 80, 114
antibacterial cream 40
anti-caking agents 33
antimicrobial materials 39
antimony trisulphide 73
appliances
 fridge freezers 88-89
 microwave ovens 78-79
 toasters 76-77
 washing machines 84-85
aqueous film-forming foam (AFFF) 119
argon 141
armour 49, 93
arsenic 83
art 54-55, 103
artificial materials
 ceramics 93
 fabrics 67
 ivory 62
 mica 108
 M sand 19
 paints 54
 rubber 45, 89, 115, 132

artificial retinas 68
artificial skin 20-21
asphalt 45, 115, 120
astronauts 132-133, 134
aviation fuel 114

B

bagasse fibre 81
bags
 fabric 66, 97
 food packaging 49, 81
 plastic 49, 146
bakeware 110
ballast 121
balloons 45, 67, 141
ballpoint pens **14-15**
balls **52-53**, 96
baseball 25, 96
baskets 66
batteries 24, 103
 hybrid cars 104, 105
 smartphone 22
 watch 16
bauxite 12
beaches 19
bearings 93
beeswax 80
belts 67, 85
beryllium 11
bicycles 12, 24, **108-109**
binoculars **112-113**
biodegradable materials 28, 60
bismuth 52
bitumen 115
body armour 49, 93
boots **42-43**, 100
BoPET 29
boron 93, 110, 112
 magnets 11, 47, 79
borosilicate glass 110, 112
bottles 29, 38, 48
bowling balls **52-53**
brakes
 bicycle 108
 car 25, 93, 105
brass 138
 musical instruments 62, 65, 83
 printers 125
 watches 17
bricks 18, 92, 143
bridges (engineering) **126-127**
bridges (musical instruments) 58, 63
bronze 83
bubbles **86-87**
bubble wrap 49, 80
building materials **142-143**
 bitumen 115
 concrete 19, 120, 121, 122
 glass 110, 135
 steel 129
 wood 61
bullet-proof vests 49

bullion 40, 134
buses 96, 102
butyl rubber 115

C

cables 10, 110, 147
camelids 97
candles 114
cans 13, 150
canvas 66
carats 68, 135
carbon 68, 128, **140**
 ballpoint pens 14
 fridge freezers 89
 mountain bikes 108-109
 nanotubes 56-57
 see also stainless steel
carbon fibre 22, 109
carbon steel 128
carborundum 32
cardboard 60, 81
carpets 67, 115, 116
cars **104-105**
 airbags 106-107
 batteries 24
 bodywork 13
 headlights 141
cashmere 97
cast iron 62
catalytic converters 104
cellulose 144
cement **120-121**, 143
 rubber 44
 sand 19
 silica 33
 see also concrete
ceramic matrix composites (CMCs) 149
ceramics **92-93**, 143, 149
 aircraft 116
 bowling balls 52
 glazes 24
 3D printers 125
 washing machines 85
chassis 129
ChemCam 130
chemical fire extinguishers 118
chemiluminescence 50
chrome 16, 58, 117
chromium 58, 77, 116
circuit boards
 copper 22, 82
 fibreglass 11, 47, 84
 gold 134
 quartz 17
 silver 41
clay **90-91**, 92, 120
clay, modelling 115
cleaning agents 102
clinker 120
clothing 66-67, 96-97, 149
 fire-proof 29, 96
 footwear 38-39, 42-43, 45

polyester 29
rubber 45
safety 48, 49, 93, 96
spacesuits 132-133
sports 40
CO_2 fire extinguishers 118
coal 45
coastal defences 121
coats 29, 97
cobalt 104, 138
coconuts 89
coins
 copper 83
 gold 134, 139
 silver 41
collagen 20, 72
colour pigments 14, 35, 54
composites **148-149**
compostable materials 81, 151
concrete 19, **120-121**, 143
 recyclable 150
 structures 122-123
 see also cement
conductive metals 11, 82, 138
construction industry 19, 143
controllers, gaming **46-47**
cookware 33, 110, 146
coolants 25, 105
copper **82-83**, 139
 aircraft 117
 cymbals 65
 fridge freezers 88
 headphones 11
 microwave ovens 79
 pianos 62
 smartphones 22
 3D printers 124
 toasters 76
corduroy 66
corn flour 106
cornstarch 81
corrosion 139
cotton 66, 80, 144
 cars 104
 money 34, 35
crayons 114
crude oil 28, 45, 48
 see also petroleum
crystals 130, 143
 silicon 32-33
 see also minerals
cupronickel 83
cups 146
cured rubber 44
Curiosity rover **130-131**
curtains 66
cut diamonds 68
cymbals 65

D

dams 121
denim 66, 103, 104
dental supplies 69, 134

INDEX

diamonds **68-69**, 93, 140
diaphragm (headphones) 11
diatomaceous earth 94
dish soap **86-87**
disposable materials 28, 29
distilled water 103
drum (musical instrument) **64-65**
drum (washing machine) 84, 85
dysprosium 105

E

earthenware 92
ebony 59
electrical connectors 10, 134
electric bikes 24
electric cars 24, **104-105**
electric guitars **58-59**
electric toasters **76-77**
electronic devices 12, 24, 32
   gaming handsets 46-47
   smartphones 22-23, 24
electronics
   microchips 19, 22, 32
   see also circuit boards
enamel 85, 94
engineered wood 61, 149
epoxy resin 101
ethylene propylene diene monomer (EPDM) 105
ethylene-tetrafluoroethylene (ETFE) resin 130
ethylene vinyl acetate (EVA) foam 39

F

fabrics **66-67**, 102, 149
   cotton 144
   laminated 38
   leather 10, 42
   nylon 6.6 107
   polyester 28-29
   recycled 104, 150
   silk 145
   spacesuits 132, 133
   wool 96-97, 145
faux diamonds 93
faux leather 10
felt 62, 96, 104
fencing 61
ferrovanadium 105
fibreboards 61
fibreglass 148
   gaming handsets 47
   skis 101
   snowboards 111
   washing machines 84
fibre-optic cables 110
fibre-reinforced materials 148, 149
fibres see fabrics
filaments 77, 124

filtration systems 18
firefighting equipment 29, 96
   extinguishers **118-119**
   retardants 74-75
fireworks 25
flax 55, 66
flooring 60
fluorescent materials 34, 51
fluoride 94, 113
foam fire extinguishers 118
foils 151
   aluminium 13, 80
   money 35
food packaging **80-81**, 141
   aluminium 13
   polyester 29
   polyethylene 49, 147
food preparation 102
football boots **42-43**
footwear 45
   football boots 42-43
   running shoes 38-39
forest fires 74
fossil fuels
   coal 45
   crude oil 28, 45, 48
   petroleum 67, 114-115
fridge freezers **88-89**
fuel 102, 114
fullerene 140
furniture 60-61, 135, 144

G

gabions 121
gallium 139
galvanized steel 85, 88
gaming handsets **46-47**
gases 48, 113, **141**
gaskets 33
gasoline 114
gears 49
gecko tape **56-57**
generators 102
gilding 135
glass 18, 24, **110-111**, 142-143
   binoculars 112
   fridge freezers 89
   glowsticks 50
   matches 72
   recyclable 150
   smartphones 23
   3D printers 125
   washing machines 84
   see also plexiglass
glass fibre 111
glassware 111
glazed ceramics 143
gloves 41, 44, 97
glowsticks **50-51**
glue 57, 72
glycerol 95
goats 67, 97, 145
gold **134-135**, 139

cars 104
   headphones 10
   smartphones 23
   spacesuits 132
gold leaf 54, 135
golf clubs 12
Gore-Tex® 132, 149
graphene 140
graphite 46, 140
gravel 18
grease 140
greenhouses 28
guanidine nitrate 106
guitars **58-59**
gum arabic 55
gutta-percha 112
gypsum 120

H

handsets, gaming **46-47**
hang gliders 29
hardwood 60
hats 96
helmets 48, 132, 134
heat transfer systems 82
helicopters 13, 25
helium 141
helmets 48, 132, 134
hide glue 72
high-density polyethylene (HDPE) 48, 147
holographic foils 35
house construction **142-143**
   bitumen 115
   concrete 19, 120, 121, 122
   glass 110, 135
   steel 129
   wood 61
household appliances
   fridge freezers 88-89
   microwave ovens 78-79
   toasters 76-77
   washing machines 84-85
human cells 20
hybrid cars **104-105**
hydrogen fuel 102

I

ice 103
ice hockey rinks 49
indium 23
industrial-grade diamonds 69
industrial solvents 103
inks 14, 34, 35
insulation materials
   aluminium 13
   glass 111
   neoprene 132
   polymers 10, 89, 147
   wool 96
iron 138
   alloys 83, 105

   see also steel
magnets 11, 47, 79
pianos 62
iron oxide 74
ivory 62

J

jackets 66
James Webb space telescope 134
jelly, petroleum 115
jets **116-117**
   engines 25, 93
jewellery
   copper 82
   diamond 68
   gold 135, 139
   silicon 32
   silver 41
jute 66

K

Kevlar® 132
keypads 41
kiln bricks 92
knives 129
krypton 141

L

lacquer 58
laminated materials 148
   fabrics 38
   glass 105, 110
   wood 100
landfill 150, 151
landscaping materials 45
lasers 130
latex 44, 112, 145
leather 67
   airbags 107
   faux 10, 147
   football boots 42
lenses 28, 110, 112-113
lepidolite 22
light bulbs 111, 141
lighting 128, 141
limestone 111, 120, 143
linear low-density polyethylene (LLDPE) 49
linen 35, 66
linseed oil 55
liquefied petroleum gas (LPG) 114
liquid crystal display (LCD) screens 125
lithium 12, **24-25**, 26-27, 117
   smartphones 22
   spacesuits 133
   watches 17
lithium-ion batteries 24, 47, 104
llamas 67, 145

INDEX

low-density polyethylene (LDPE) 49, 147
  bubble wrap 80
  fridge freezers 89
LPG 114
lubricants 15, 114, 139

M

magnesium 112, 113
magnets
  electric guitars 58, 59
  gaming handsets 47
  headphones 11
  microwave ovens 78, 79
mahogany 58
manufactured sand (M sand) 19
Mars rovers 13, **130-131**
matches **72-73**
medical supplies
  artificial skin 20-21
  gold 135
  lithium 25
  polyester 28
  prosthetics 68, 93, 140
  silver 40
  water 103
medium-density polyethylene (MDPE) 48
membrane switches 41
metals **138-139**
  aluminium 12-13
  copper 82-83
  gold 134-135
  lithium 24-25
  recyclable 150
  silver 40-41
  see also steel
mica 77, 79, 108
microchips 19, 22, 32
microfibre cloths 29
microspheres 26
microwave ovens **78-79**
milk pasteurization 102
minerals
  diamonds 68-69, 93, 140
  quartz 16-17, 131
  see also crystals
mirrors 40, 134
mohair 97
money **34-35**
monomers 146-147
mortar 18, 120
mother-of-pearl 59
mountain bikes **108-109**
musical instruments 83, 139
  drum kits 64-65
  electric guitars 58-59
  pianos 62-63
  see also headphones

N

nanoparticles 39, 135
nano tape **56-57**
naphtha 115
natural materials **144-145**
  ceramics 92
  diamonds 68-69

paints 54
plastics 28
quartz 16-17, 131
rubber 44
sand 18, 19
silicon 32-33
wood 60-61
see also fossil fuels
Neodymium
  lasers 130
  magnets 11, 47, 79
neon signs 141
neoprene 45, 132
netting 81
nichrome 77
nickel 83, 138
  aircraft 116
  electric guitars 59
  smartphones 22
  toasters 77
nitrogen gas 104, 107, 113
noble gases **141**
Nomex® 132
non-oxide ceramics 93
nut shells 105
nylon
  balloons 67
  bicycle saddles 108
  pins (bowling) 53
  spacesuits 133
  toothbrushes 95
nylon 6.6 yarn 107, 147

O

obscure glass 111
ocean beds 19
oil, crude 28, 45, 48
  see also petroleum
oil, linseed 55
oleic acid 15
ovens, microwave **78-79**

P

packaging, food **80-81**, 141
  aluminium 13
  polyester 29
  polyethylene 49, 147
paints 18, **54-55**, 103
paper 60, 81, 103
  see also money
paraffin 73, 100, 114
particle-reinforced composites 148
pasteurization 102
pens, ballpoint **14-15**
peppermint 94
periodic table 141
pesticides 83
petroleum 67, **114-115**
  see also crude oil
petroleum jelly 115
phenyl oxalate ester 51
phones **22-23**, 24, 41
phosphorus 73
phosphorescence 16
pianos **62-63**
pickups 58, 59

pigments 14, 54
pipes 82, 88, 147
plant-based fabrics 66
plasma 141
plaster 19, 120, 142
plastic bags 49
plasticine 115
plastics 139
  ABS 89, 112
  fire extinguishers 119
  glowsticks 50
  headphones 10
  nylon 6.6 107, 147
  polycarbonate 116
  polyester 28-29
  polyethylene 48-49, 80, 147
  polylactic acid (PLA) 124
  polypropylene 76, 79, 104
  polyurethane 43, 89
  polyvinyl chloride (PVC) 85, 147
  recycled 17, 38, 151
  reinforced 149
  skis 100
  spacesuits 133
plating 59, 134
playground equipment 48
pleather 10
plexiglass 16
ploughs 128
plumbing supplies 33, 48, 82
plutonium-238 131
plywood 61, 149
PMMA (plexiglass) 16
polish 69
polyacrylonitrile (PAN) 109
polycarbonates 28, 146
  aircraft 116
  gaming handsets 46
polycrystalline diamonds (PCD) 69
polyester **28-29**
  clothing 42
  drums 65
  footwear 38
polyethylene **48-49**, 146, 147
  fridge freezers 89
  packaging 80
  skis 100
polyethylene terephthalate (PET) 29
polyimide film 131
polylactic acid (PLA) 124
polymers **146-147**
polypropylene 115
  cars 104
  microwave ovens 79
  toasters 76
polystyrene 115, 146
  fridge freezers 88
  packaging 81
polytetrafluoroethylene 132
polyurethane
  boots 42, 100
  bowling balls 53
  fridge freezers 89
  headphones 10
polyvinyl butyral (PVB) 105
polyvinyl chloride (PVC) 147

headphones 10
3D printers 125
toasters 77
washing machines 85
porcelain 33, 85, 92
potassium chlorate 72
potentiometers 46
pottery materials **90-91**, 92
powder fire extinguishers 118
power lines 12
pre-cast concrete 121
printers **124-125**
propellers 83
prosthetics 68, 93, 140
  skin 20-21
pulped wood 60, 81
pulp, paper 81, 103
purification systems 40, 83
PVC see polyvinyl chloride (PVC)

Q

quarries 19, 92
quartz **16-17**, 131

R

racing cars 25
radiation-resistant materials 110, 130
radon 141
rayon 60
rebar 128
rechargeable batteries 23, 24, 104
record players 69
recyclable materials **150-151**
  concrete 121
  fabrics 104
  paper pulp 81
  plastics 17, 38, 48-49
  rubber 45
red phosphorus 73
refined petroleum 114
reflective materials 86, 113, 132
refractory materials 92
refrigerant 88
reinforced materials 148
  concrete 120, 122
  glass 111
  plastics 22, 117, 149
  rubber 119
resins
  bowling balls 53
  cars 105
  electric guitars 58
  skis 101
retardants, fire **74-75**
roads 45, 120
rockets 93, 129
Roman concrete 121
roofing materials 115, 121, 142
rosewood 59
rubber **44-45**, 115, 145
  bicycles 109
  binoculars 112, 113
  cars 104, 105
  fire extinguishers 119
  football boots 43

INDEX

fridge freezers 89
microwave ovens 78
running shoes 39
skis 101
spacesuits 132
washing machines 84
ruby 125
rugs 67
running shoes **38-39**
see also football boots

S

safety equipment 48, 49, 96
   fire extinguishers 118-119
   fire-proximity suits 29
   fire retardants 74-75
   helmets 48, 132, 134
   spacesuits 132-133
salt flats 26-27
sand **18-19**
sandblasting 19
sanitary ware 92
sauces 102
scarves 97
screens 110, 125
   touchscreens 23, 41
sculpture 103
seagrass 66
sealants 33
security threads 34
sensors 46, 106
serial numbers 34
setae 57
sheep 67, 96
shells 59
ship locks **122-123**
shirts 66
shoelaces 39, 42
shoes, running **38-39**
   see also football boots
silica 33, 110
silicon **32-33**
   airbags 107
   artificial skin 20
   microchips 22
   sun cream 26
   wafers 19, 32
   watches 17
silicone 33, 107, 146
silk 29, 67, 145
silt 18
silumin 32
silver 23, 39, **40-41**
skiing **100-101**
skin, artificial **20-21**
skin creams 115
smartphones **22-23**, 24, 41
smart TVs 110
snowboards 111
soap **86-87**
soapstone 77
soda-lime glass 111
sodium lauryl sulphate 95
sodium salicylate 51
softwood 61
solar panels 32, 41, 111
solder 139
solvents 103

spacecraft 13, 93, **130-131**
spacesuits **132-133**
space telescopes 134
spandex 67, 133
sports
   clothing 29, 40, 67
   equipment 12, 111, 149
   football boots 42-43
   pitches 45, 49
   running shoes 38-39
   skiing 100-101
spruce 63
stainless steel 129, 139
   airbags 106
   bicycles 109
   microwave ovens 79
   skis 100
   3D printers 125
   washing machines 85
statues 83
steam 102
steatite 77
steel **128-129**, 139
   aircraft 117
   bridges 126-127
   cars 104
   electric guitars 59
   fridge freezers 88
   galvanized steel 85, 88
   microwave ovens 78
   pianos 62
   spacecraft 130
   toasters 76
   washing machines 85
   see also stainless steel
sterilization 103
sterling silver 41
stibnite 73
sticky materials 56-57
stoneware 92
strontium 16
stucco plaster 120
studs 43
sugar cane 80-81
sun cream **26-27**
sustainable materials
   biodegradable materials 28, 60
   compostable materials 81, 151
   see also recyclable materials
synthetic materials
   ceramics 93
   fabrics 67
   ivory 62
   mica 108
   M sand 19
   paints 54
   rubber 45, 89, 115, 132

T

talcum powder 106
telescopes 130, 134
tempera paints 54
tempered glass 84, 89
tents 66
terracotta 92
Terylene® 28
textile recycling 150

textiles
   see also fabrics
thermometers 139
thermoplastic polyurethane (TPU) 43
thermoplastics 46, 59, 124
   see also polycarbonates
thermosetting polymers 146
thermosoftening polymers 146
   3D printers **124-125**
   3D steel bridge **126-127**
ties 67
timber 61
tin 23
titanium 117, 131
toasters **76-77**
tools 69, 129, 140
toothbrushes 147
toothpaste **94-95**
touchscreens 23, 41
toys 33, 49, 60
trains 13, 128
transportation
   aircraft 13, 116-117, 139
   bicycles 12, 24, 108-109
   buses 96, 102
   helicopters 13, 25
   spacecraft 13, 93, 130-131
   trains 13, 128
   see also cars
trousers 66
tungsten 14, 22
tunnels 121
turbines 102
turntables 69, 78
TVs 110
tyres 44-45, 108, 145

U

ultra-high-molecular-weight polyethylene (UHMWPE) 49
ultra-high-temperature ceramics (UHTCs) 143
ultraviolet (UV) materials 34
uncured rubber 44
upright pianos **62-63**
urethane 52
   see also polyurethane
utensils 60, 139

V

velvet 66
veneers 53, 60, 62
voice coils 11, 47

W

wafers, silicon 32
washing machines **84-85**
waste 38, 104, 150-151
watches **16-17**
water 38, **102-103**
watercolours 55
water filtration 18
water fire extinguishers 118
waterproof materials
   beeswax 80

concrete 121
glass 110
Gore-Tex® 132, 149
metals 85
plastic 17, 28, 115
rubber 39
silicone 33
water purification 40
water-resistant materials 38, 143, 148
wax 80, 100, 114
wetsuits 45
window frames 12
windows
   acrylic 116
   glass 110, 111, 135
   metals 12
   plastics 28, 146
wire coatings 49, 125
wiring 79, 82
wood **60-61**, 144, 149
   electric guitars 58-59
   matches 72
   packaging 81
   pianos 62, 63
   pins (bowling) 53
   recycling 150
   skis 100
   3D printers 124
wool 67, **96-97**, 145
   aircraft 116
   insulation 111
   pianos 62
   steel 128

X

xenon 141
x-rays 40

Y

yarn 66, 96, 107

Z

zinc 83, 139
   cymbals 65
   galvanized steel 85

ACKNOWLEDGMENTS

DK would like to thank: Sarah Bailey, Abhijit Dutta, Becca Fry, and Janashree Singha for editorial assistance; Diya Varma for help with the illustrations; Revati Anand for help with jacket design; Jim Green for design assistance; Rakesh Kumar for jacket finishes; Samrajkumar S for picture research administration; Peter Gee for proofreading; and Elizabeth Wise for the index.

The publisher would like to thank the following for their kind permission to reproduce their photographs:
(Key: a-above; b-below/bottom; c-centre; f-far; l-left; r-right; t-top)

5 Dreamstime.com: Vvoevale (crb). **TurboSquid:** ArtGraphic3d Studio (cb). **6 Dreamstime.com:** Hlubokidzianis (tl); Macrovector Art (bc); Taslim Uddin (cl); Icons Home cl (bulb); Artur Kutskyi (c); Tarikvision (c/lady); Macrovector Art (crb); Macrovector (cra/tree, cra). **7 Dreamstime.com:** Oleh Ilechko (tr); Tele52 (tl); Golden Sikorka (c); Golden Sikorka (bl); Tarikvision (br). **8 Dreamstime.com:** Christian Jung (br). **Shutterstock.com:** Cat Us (cla). **9 Dreamstime.com:** Ajijchan (cra); Jozsef Soos (tl); Song Heming (tc/Fireworks); Niphon Sangwanmanon (tr); Martin Konopka (fbl); Luyag2 (bl); Petr Malyshev (bc); Guo Wei (br); Toxitz (fbr). **Getty Images / iStock:** South_agency (tc). **10 Dreamstime.com:** Nebojsa Babic (br). **11 Dreamstime.com:** Bwylezich (bl). **Getty Images / iStock:** RHJ (ca). **12 Adobe Stock:** Svetlana Gryankina (bc); Michael (clb). **Dreamstime.com:** Pepebaeza (bl); Cagkan Sayin (tr); Korn Vitthayanukarun (ca); Wdnetagency (cla). **Shutterstock.com:** Nejron Photo (cb). **12-13 Getty Images / iStock:** E+ / Kerrick (c). **13 Dreamstime.com:** Anidimi (tr); Cbechinie (tl); Srki66 (tc); Ryan Fletcher (c); Oleksandr Kulik (bc); Boarding1now (bl). **Getty Images / iStock:** MyrKu (cra). **NASA:** JPL-Caltech / ASU / MSSS (crb). **14 Dreamstime.com:** Ajijchan (cl). **Shutterstock.com:** AkulininaOlga (bl). **14-15 Alamy Stock Photo:** imageBROKER / alimdi / Matthias Lenke. **15 Dreamstime.com:** Christian Jung (tc). **16 Dorling Kindersley:** Ruth Jenkinson / RGB Research Limited (cb). **TurboSquid:** DIC3D_Models (tr). **17 Alamy Stock Photo:** Emy Maike (br). **Dreamstime.com:** Peter Hermes Furian (cra). **TurboSquid:** DIC3D_Models. **18 Dreamstime.com:** Aucher Mathieu (tc); Nordroden (cla); Ivonne Wierink (crb); Photka (c). **Getty Images / iStock:** Maya Shustov (cl). **Shutterstock.com:** Ivan4es (cb). **19 Dreamstime.com:** Chormail (tl); Mtayfunseker (clb); Dmitry Kalinovsky (ca); Nordroden (cra); Domnitsky (c); Moreno Soppelsa (bc); Wirestock (bc/Ocean); Halpand (br). **20-21 Science Photo Library:** Mauro Fermariello. **22 Adobe Stock:** Henri Koskinen (tl). **Getty Images / iStock:** Wongsakorn Napaeng (bl). **23 Dreamstime.com:** Björn Wylezich (tr). **24 Adobe Stock:** Martinlisner (bc); Sergey Ryzhov (tr). **Alamy Stock Photo:** Westend61 GmbH / Andrés Benitez (cl). **Dreamstime.com:** Alexander Dorn (tc); Anatolii Savitskii (tl); Petr Malyshev (ca); Oksana Ermak (c); Olga Ovchinnikova (br). **Science Photo Library:** (cla). **24-25 Dreamstime.com:** Björn Wylezich (ca). **25 Alamy Stock Photo:** David James (bc); JG Photography (ca). **Dreamstime.com:** Song Heming (bl); Jozsef Soos (tr); Lightpainter (cra); Methaphum Thongbun (crb). **Getty Images:** Icon Sportswire (c); Gaston Brito Miserocchi (clb). **26-27 Tom Hegen:** The Lithium Series. **28 Dreamstime.com:** Allexxandar (br); Sergey201982 (ca); Sergey Novikov (c); Pixura (bl); Guo Wei (crb). **Shutterstock.com:** Cat Us (tr). **29 Adobe Stock:** Brainiac (tr). **Dreamstime.com:** Kawaiikavachay (cla); Norgal (ca); Kritchanut (cr); Niphon Sangwanmanon (bl); Waihs (br). **Getty Images / iStock:** E+ / Hanis (cra); South_agency (bc). **Shutterstock.com:** Hari Nurosid (c). **30-31 Science Photo Library:** Steve Gschmeissner. **32 Adobe Stock:** Amazing Studio (br). **Dreamstime.com:** Rozaliya (tl); Björn Wylezich (ca). **Getty Images / iStock:** E+ / Nimis69 (cra); Artur Slobodian (cl); E+ / Eloi_Omella (cb). **32-33 Dreamstime.com:** Martin Konopka (c). **33 Adobe Stock:** DmyTo (br); Markuso (ca); Allen Penton (cra). **Dreamstime.com:** Altinosmanaj (tl); Photomall (tc); Roberto Junior (tr); Luyag2 (c); Oksix (clb); Toa555 (crb); Wirestock (bl); Toxitz (bc). **34 Adobe Stock:** Nmann77 (tl). **Shutterstock.com:** Holger Kleine (bc). **34-35 Adobe Stock:** Deviddo. **35 Alamy Stock Photo:** Leonid Serebrennikov (br). **Dreamstime.com:** Dariusz Kopestynski (bl). **36 Dreamstime.com:** Itsmejust (br); Björn Wylezich (cla). **37 Adobe Stock:** Dzain (tr). **Alamy Stock Photo:** Andy Selinger (tc). **Dreamstime.com:** Chernetskaya (bl); Anton Starikov (cla); Paul Topp (tl); Björn Wylezich (bc); Igor Kaliuzhnyi (br); Viktoriya Kuzmenkova (fbr). **Getty Images / iStock:** Supersmario (cra). **38 Dreamstime.com:** Stockcreations (crb). **39 Dreamstime.com:** Bwylezich (tr). **Science Photo Library:** Stefan Diller (bl). **40 Alamy Stock Photo:** Science Photo Library / Kateryna Kon (cb); Science History Images / Photo Researchers (bc). **Dreamstime.com:** Alexkalina (bl); Volodymyr Pishchanyi (tr); Itsmejust (ca); Daniela Spyropoulou (cl). **The Metropolitan Museum of Art:** Rogers Fund, 1907 (tc). **40-41 Dreamstime.com:** Björn Wylezich (c). **41 Alamy Stock Photo:** PjrStudio (ca). **Dreamstime.com:** Andrii Hasiuk (tl); Malkeet Singh (tc); Natallia Khlapushyna (tr); Photovova (cb); Danny Raustadt (bc); Viktoriya Kuzmenkova (br). **Shutterstock.com:** FatihYavuz (cr). **42 Shutterstock.com:** FatihYavuz (bl); RHJPhtotos (br). **42-43 Getty Images:** Jam Media. **44 Alamy Stock Photo:** Andy Selinger (crb); Wavebreak Media Premium / Wavebreakmedia Ltd UC32 (cla). **Dreamstime.com:** Maksym Dragunov (cra); Toa555 (ca); Anton Starikov (clb); Michael Turner (bc); Antonio Guillem (bl). **45 Alamy Stock Photo:** Tetra Images, LLC / Inti St Clair (tl). **Dreamstime.com:** Chernetskaya (cb); Mheim301165 (tr); Paul Topp (ca); Ozgur Coskun (crb); Ilya Zaytsev (bc). **Shutterstock.com:** Knyazevfoto (clb); zzphoto.ru (tc); Val Lawless (cra). **46 Dreamstime.com:** Stanislau V (cl). **47 Science Photo Library:** Biophoto Associates (bl). **48 Adobe Stock:** Irina (cra). **Alamy Stock Photo:** Steve Lindridge (crb). **Dreamstime.com:** Viorel Dudau (bl); Darko Sreckovic (tr); Andrey Khokhlov (ca); Megaflopp (cl); Richardjohnsonuk (cb). **Getty Images / iStock:** Ktmophoto (bc). **49 Adobe Stock:** Givaga (clb). **Dreamstime.com:** Ale059 (crb); Vladwitty (tl); Stanislau V (cla); Stocksnapper (ca); Mrmrsmarcha (c); Rwb (cb). **Getty Images / iStock:** Alan64 (bc); Luhuanfeng (tc); Jose Luis Carrascosa (br). **Shutterstock.com:** Emasali Stock (cra). **50-51 Adobe Stock:** Bluesnote. **51 Adobe Stock:** Jeffrey Daly (cra). **52 Dreamstime.com:** Björn Wylezich (bl). **Getty Images:** Bloomberg (tl). **53 Depositphotos Inc:** Borjomi88 (cr). **Getty Images:** Bloomberg (clb). **54 Alamy Stock Photo:** Megan Kobe (bl). **Los Angeles County Museum of Art:** Neri Di Bicci (cra). **Shutterstock.com:** Pixparts (crb); Becky Starsmore (clb). **54-55 Dreamstime.com:** Torsakarin (Background). **55 Dreamstime.com:** Luis

ACKNOWLEDGMENTS

Echeverri Urrea (cr). **Getty Images / iStock:** 3sbworld (tr); Strelov (tc); Lvenks (cla). **Shutterstock.com:** Sofia Voronkova (b). **56-57 Science Photo Library:** Eye of Science (t). **57 Alamy Stock Photo:** Science History Images / Photo Researchers (crb). **Dreamstime.com:** Good Dreams Studio (br). **Shutterstock.com:** Koosen (bc). **58 Alamy Stock Photo:** Amilciar Gualdron (tr). **Getty Images / iStock:** E+ / RyanJLane (br). **60 123RF.com:** Anton Starikov (bc). **Alamy Stock Photo:** POL / BT (br). **Dreamstime.com:** Anikasalsera (tl); Costasz (tc); Anikasalsera (tr); Hein Teh (ca); Pixelrobot (cl); Siamnugkhathut Purathaka (clb). **Shutterstock.com:** Chad Robertson Media (cr). **61 Alamy Stock Photo:** Avalon / Construction Photography (ca); Eden Breitz (tc); Zbynek Pospisil (bc). **Dreamstime.com:** Megamnogo (cl). **Getty Images:** Bloomber (cb). **Getty Images / iStock:** Gmnicholas (br); Iiievgeniy (cr). **62-63 TurboSquid:** Theowithoutdor. **62 Dreamstime.com:** Jatuporn79 (bl). **63 Alamy Stock Photo:** World Photography Archiv (cr). **64-65 Shutterstock.com:** Dmytro Vietrov. **66 Adobe Stock:** Tarzhanova (clb). **Dreamstime.com:** Peter Cripps (tl); Paul Loewen (ca); Jcsmilly (cb); Maxine Hovell (bc). **Getty Images / iStock:** Al62 (cra); Garry518 (tc); Dogayusufdokdok (cla); Liujunrong (crb). **67 Adobe Stock:** Dzain (br); Javier (tc). **Dreamstime.com:** Viktor Nikitin (bc); Phang Kim Shan (ca); Pavalache Stelian (c). **Getty Images / iStock:** Foto-Video-Studio (clb); Supersmario (tl). **Shutterstock.com:** Kostiantyn Ablazov (cra). **68 Alamy Stock Photo:** Sergio Azenha (cl). **Dreamstime.com:** Igor Kaliuzhnyi (cla); Chalermpon Poungpeth (tl); Luchschen (cr). **Science Photo Library:** Look at Sciences / Patrice Latron (cra). **69 Alamy Stock Photo:** Science History Images (clb). **Dreamstime.com:** Anzhelika Bosak (cb); Konstik (tc); Orcea David (tr). **Getty Images / iStock:** Angelika-Angelika (ca). **Science Photo Library:** Martin Bond (bl); Dirk Wiersma (cla). **Shutterstock.com:** Sfrolov (cr). **70 Alamy Stock Photo:** Pixel-shot / Leonid Iastremskyi (cl). **Shutterstock.com:** Robilad Co (br). **TurboSquid:** ArtGraphic3d Studio (cb); munal3d (bc); mrgrotey (clb). **71 123RF.com:** Karandaev (br). **Alamy Stock Photo:** Associated Press / Noah Berger (bl). **Dreamstime.com:** All Music Instruments Photos (fbr); Tetiana Kovalenko (ftl); Sakchaiphoto (tr); Nayneung1 (cra); Hapelena (fbl); Shawn Hempel (bc). **Getty Images:** Jeff Spicer / BAFTA (tc). **Shutterstock.com:** TorriPhoto (tl). **72 Kyle Riding and Mohammadreza Mirzahosseini:** (ca). **Shutterstock.com:** Angela M. Benivegna (tr). **72-73 Alamy Stock Photo:** Pixel-shot / Leonid Iastremskyi. **73 Alamy Stock Photo:** Phil Degginger (tl). **Dorling Kindersley:** Ruth Jenkinson / RGB Research Limited (cr). **74-75 Alamy Stock Photo:** Associated Press / Noah Berger. **76 TurboSquid:** munal3d (bc). **76-77 TurboSquid:** ArtGraphic3d Studio (c). **77 Alamy Stock Photo:** Phil Degginger (cra). **Dreamstime.com:** Evgenii Kharitonov (br); Korn Vitthayanukarun (tl). **TurboSquid:** mrgrotey (crb). **78 Alamy Stock Photo:** PA Images / Nick Ansell (cl). **79 Depositphotos Inc:** leungchopan (tc). **Shutterstock.com:** Real Waseem Khan (bl). **80 Dreamstime.com:** Chernetskaya (tl); Guo Wei (tr); Nayneung1 (c); Stocksnapper (bl). **81 Dreamstime.com:** Candy1812 (cb); Korn Vitthayanukarun (tl); Olga Kovalenko (tr); Shawn Hempel (cr); Sakchaiphoto (clb); Italianestro (b). **82 Dreamstime.com:** Oleg Doroshin (clb); Kirill Makarov (tr); Wirestock (c); Arnis Rukis (bl); Peter Hermes Furian (cb); Vvoevale (cr). **Shutterstock.com:** Shutter Baby photo (br). **83 Alamy Stock Photo:** Adam Eastland (crb). **Dreamstime.com:** All Music Instruments Photos (cr); Andrei Kuzmik (tl); Tetiana Kovalenko (bl); Suvit Maka (bc). **Getty Images:** Jeff Spicer / BAFTA (c); Bloomberg (tc). **Getty Images / iStock:** herstockart (tr). **85 Dreamstime.com:** Mulderphoto (br); Shamils (tr). **Shutterstock.com:** Dinga (bl). **86-87 Shutterstock.com:** TorriPhoto. **88 Dreamstime.com:** Hapelena (tl). **89 123RF.com:** Karandaev (fbr). **Dorling Kindersley:** Ruth Jenkinson / RGB Research Limited (br). **Dreamstime.com:** Robert309 (tr). **90-91 Shutterstock.com:** Robilad Co. **92 Alamy Stock Photo:** funkyfood London - Paul Williams (bl). **Dreamstime.com:** Chernetskaya (bc); Zzz1b (tl); Alexander Levchenko (tc); Diianadimitrova (ca); Madrugadaverde (cl); Kpoppie (cr); NatashaBreen (cb). **93 Alamy Stock Photo:** Sylvie Pabion (bl). **Dreamstime.com:** Martin Brayley (cra); Andrey Simonenko (tc); Chernetskaya (cl); Emma Ros (br). **Getty Images / iStock:** RoMiEg (crb); Sunshower Shots (c). **Science Photo Library:** Eye Of Science (ca); Power And Syred (cb). **Shutterstock.com:** alvant (tl). **94 Dreamstime.com:** Thananya Karnjanaphast (bl). **Getty Images / iStock:** RusN (tr). **Science Photo Library:** Dennis Kunkel Microscopy (cl). **94-95 Dreamstime.com:** Chernetskaya. **96 Adobe Stock:** ChiccoDodiFC (bl). **Dreamstime.com:** Helga11 (tr); Peerapong Peattayakul (cla); Ksena2009 (cb); Ronstik (bc). **Getty Images / iStock:** Semen Salivanchuk (tc); SeventyFour (crb). **Getty Images:** Tom Szczerbowski (cl). **Shutterstock.com:** Naruedom Yaempongsa (c). **97 Adobe Stock:** Pavel Svoboda (clb). **Dreamstime.com:** Yehoshua Halevi (cra); Slowmotiongli (tl). **Getty Images:** Bloomberg (bc). **Getty Images / iStock:** consulgian (cr); Tarzhanova (c). **Shutterstock.com:** PanSvitlyna (br). **98 Dreamstime.com:** Jaroslav Moravcik (cla). **99 Alamy Stock Photo:** Yuen Man Cheung (fbl); Science History Images / Photo Researchers (cra); The Consoli Collection (fbr). **Dreamstime.com:** Praethip Docekalova (cla); Iamtkb (tc); Pedro Nogueira (bc). **Shutterstock.com:** asharkyu (bl); Benoit Daoust (tl). **TurboSquid:** CREO with Chris (br). **100 Dreamstime.com:** Aleksandr Potashev (clb). **Getty Images / iStock:** E+ / ArtistGNDphotography (bc). **100-101 Alamy Stock Photo:** Mauro Dalla Pozza. **101 Getty Images / iStock:** Hydrogenn (br). **102 Alamy Stock Photo:** fStop Images GmbH / Ableimages (ca); RGtimeline (clb); RossHelen editorial (bl). **Dreamstime.com:** Alexander Hoffmann (cr); Margaryta Vakhterova (ftr); Scharfsinn86 (tr); Viktor Kanunnikov (bc). **Getty Images:** Moment / Vithun Khamsong (cb). **Getty Images / iStock:** YelenaYemchuk (cla). **103 Alamy Stock Photo:** H. Mark Weidman Photography (tc). **Dreamstime.com:** Antoniodiaz (cr); Apichart Teapakdee (tr); Ggw1962 (ca); Igor Zakharevich (c); Anne Richard (cb); Moreno Soppelsa (bl). **Getty Images / iStock:** megaflopp (tl). **Shutterstock.com:** Forance (bc). **104-105 TurboSquid:** qapqor. **104 Alamy Stock Photo:** Sahadat Hossain (tl). **Dreamstime.com:** Bwylezich (bc). **105 Dreamstime.com:** Tetiana Kovalenko (br). **106 Dreamstime.com:** Kuprevich (tr). **107 Dreamstime.com:** Aleksandar Varbenov (tl). **108 Shutterstock.com:** Lea Rae (cl). **109 Dreamstime.com:** Alex Gor (br). **Shutterstock.com:** Composite_Carbonman (tr). **110 Alamy Stock Photo:** Sipa US

ACKNOWLEDGMENTS

(cra). **Dreamstime.com:** Destina156 (tc); Iuliia Nedrygailova (c); Nichibus (cb); Oleg Miasin (br). **Getty Images / iStock:** Michael Blann (cr). **Shutterstock.com:** asharkyu (bc). **111 Alamy Stock Photo:** The Consoli Collection (tr). **Dreamstime.com:** Denis Babenko (br); Rose-marie Henriksson (tl); Alpar Benedek (ca); Xxlphoto (cb); Dpproductions (cr). **Shutterstock.com:** Benoit Daoust (cl); irin-k (bc). **112-113 TurboSquid:** ArtGraphic3d Studio. **112 Dreamstime.com:** Bwylezich (tr); Toon Sang (tl). **113 Dreamstime.com:** Viktorfischer (cr). **Shutterstock.com:** Margoe Edwards (bc). **114 Adobe Stock:** dean (cl). **Alamy Stock Photo:** Radharc Images (crb). **Dreamstime.com:** Tetiana Kovalenko (cb); Andrey Popov (fcra); VanderWolfImages (c); Pedro Nogueira (bl). **Getty Images / iStock:** Albina Gavrilovic (tr); Taitai6769 (bc). **Science Photo Library:** VICTOR DE SCHWANBERG (cra). **115 Dreamstime.com:** Chernetskaya (tl); Tatiana Muslimova (tc); Kosovskyi (tr); Nyul (crb); Madhourse (bl); Praethip Docekalova (c). **Getty Images / iStock:** Sergii Petruk (cb). **Shutterstock.com:** Margoe Edwards (cr). **116-117 TurboSquid:** 3d_molier International. **116 Science Photo Library:** EYE OF SCIENC (clb). **TurboSquid:** CREO with Chris (br). **117 Science Photo Library:** PHIL DEGGINGER (bl). **118 Adobe Stock:** Maksym Yemelyanov (bl). **118-119 Getty Images / iStock:** Diy13. **119 Getty Images / iStock:** Sviatlana Lazarenka (tl). **120-121 Alamy Stock Photo:** Zoonar GmbH (ca). **120 Alamy Stock Photo:** Bonita Cheshier (tc). **Dreamstime.com:** Bogdanhoda (cr); Plotnikov (cl); Monikabaumbach (crb). **Getty Images / iStock:** Canetti (ca); i-Stockr (br). **121 Adobe Stock:** Alexander Erdbeer (ca). **Alamy Stock Photo:** qaphotos.com (c); Justin Kase zsixz (cra). **Dreamstime.com:** Dark Caramel (clb); Lukasz Kielas (tl); SensejG (tr); Wirestock (bl); Chandrasekhar Velayudhan (bc); Mishkacz (br). **122-123 Getty Images:** VCG. **124 Dreamstime.com:** Jeevan Gb (tl). **125 Dreamstime.com:** Iamtkb (bl). **Science Photo Library:** KARL GAFF (tr). **126-127 Dreamstime.com:** Andrew Balcombe. **128 Dreamstime.com:** Eternalfeelings (cb); Yang Yu (tr); Nuttawut Uttamaharad (c). **Getty Images / iStock:** simonkr (ca). **Shutterstock.com:** Jannarong (cr). **129 Alamy Stock Photo:** Connect Images (clb); yos_moes (tl); JRC, Inc. (tc); NurPhoto SRL (cr); imageBROKER.com (crb). **Dreamstime.com:** Radzh Dzhabbarov (cla). **Getty Images:** Srinophan69 (bc). **Shutterstock.com:** pisaphotography (c). **131 Alamy Stock Photo:** Science History Images / Photo Researchers (tl). **Science Photo Library:** NREL / US Department Of Energy (br). **132 Adobe Stock:** Katarina (clb). **Dorling Kindersley:** Colin Keates / Natural History Museum, London (tl). **Getty Images / iStock:** gerenme (cla). **134 Adobe Stock:** Designpics (cla). **Alamy Stock Photo:** NASA / Pictorial Press Ltd (tc); Claude Thibault (cl). **Dreamstime.com:** Hdesert (clb); Sovpag (bl); Ismail Rabbani Rajo (cb); Kevkhiev Yury (bc); Steveheap (tr). **Getty Images:** Bloomberg / Victor J. Blue (c). **134-135 Alamy Stock Photo:** Yuen Man Cheung (c). **135 Adobe Stock:** romaset (br). **Alamy Stock Photo:** Quentin Bargate (crb); Photononstop / Philippe Turpin (c). **Dreamstime.com:** Ozgur Guvenc (ca); Jaroslav Moravcik (tc). **136 Alamy Stock Photo:** Tetra Images (c). **Dreamstime.com:** Orlando Jose De Castro Junior (bc); Stevanovicigor (crb). **137 123RF.com:** Aleksey Poprugin (fbl). **Adobe Stock:** shutnica (tc). **Dreamstime.com:** Hugoht (cla); Thelightwriter (tl); Netfalls (cra); Roberto Junior (bc); Dmitry Markov (fbr). **Getty Images / iStock:** vchal (bl). **138 Adobe Stock:** master1305 (bc). **Dreamstime.com:** Kalcutta (br); Stevanovicigor (bl); Anna Kreichman (bc/gold). **139 Adobe Stock:** Sylvie Thenard (cr/thermomètre). **Dreamstime.com:** Steven Arnold (c); Orlando Jose De Castro Junior (cl); Netfalls (cra); Jiri Novotny (cr); Breakermaximus (crb). **Getty Images / iStock:** E+ / Trawick-Images (c/coins); ronstik (br). **140 Dreamstime.com:** Amrkl5 (clb); Roberto Junior (cl); Thelightwriter (c); Vvoevale (cr); Dmitry Markov (bl). **Shutterstock.com:** algae (clb/grease); Viktor Loki (fcr). **141 Alamy Stock Photo:** CB Still Life (br); Tetra Images (cr). **Dreamstime.com:** Chernetskaya (cr/veggies); Serhii Moiseiev (cra); Scanrail (crb). **Getty Images / iStock:** vchal (cl). **Shutterstock.com:** ClaudioValdes (crb/bulbs). **142 Shutterstock.com:** berni0004. **143 Alamy Stock Photo:** Findlay (bl). **Dreamstime.com:** Aksakalko (clb); Serhii Ivashchuk (cl); Kinek00 (br). **144 Adobe Stock:** shutnica (br). **Dreamstime.com:** Paul Loewen (bl); Tyler Olson (cl); Rodho (cr). **145 Alamy Stock Photo:** Riccardo Sala (cl). **Dreamstime.com:** Hugoht (bl); Toon Sang (tl); Photodynamx (tr); Malgorzata Kistryn (cr). **Getty Images / iStock:** Oleg_Ermak (br). **146 123RF.com:** Aleksey Poprugin (br). **Dreamstime.com:** Alexander Donin (bc); Bowonpat Sakaew (clb); Eugenesergeev (cb); Isaac Hughes (bl). **147 Dreamstime.com:** Francesco Marzovillo (tr); Velmen12 (cb). **148 Shutterstock.com:** Composite_Carbonman (c). **149 Dreamstime.com:** Andrew Angelov (bl); Lachris77 (tl); Adrian Luca (tc); Ileana Marcela Bosogea Tudor (tc/coffin); Wabeno (br). **The Metropolitan Museum of Art:** Rogers Fund, 1935 (tr). **Science Photo Library:** Eye Of Science (cr). **150 Adobe Stock:** Belish (c); ungvar (bl). **Dreamstime.com:** David Burke (cl); Chernetskaya (cr); Mohammed Anwarul Kabir Choudhury (bc). **Shutterstock.com:** Maksim Safaniuk (br). **151 Dreamstime.com:** Wachiwit (bl). **Science Photo Library:** Nancy J. Pierce (br)

Cover images: *Front:* **123RF.com:** Anton Starikov tl; **Adobe Stock:** Designpics cra; **Alamy Stock Photo:** Yuen Man Cheung cr, Nathaniel Noir cb, Björn Wylezich fcra; **Dreamstime.com:** Jatuporn79 fclb, Igor Kaliuzhnyi ca/ (diamond), Tetiana Kovalenko br, Viktor Nikitin clb, Toon Sang cla/ (latex), Nuttawut Uttamaharad ca, Vvoevale ftl; **Getty Images:** Moment / Maciej Toporowicz, NYC tc; **Getty Images / iStock:** Tarzhanova crb/ (scarf); **Shutterstock.com:** Sebastian Janicki bc, NewFabrika ftr, Hari Nurosid crb; **TurboSquid:** ArtGraphic3d Studio cla, fbl, DIC3D_Models tr, mrgrotey bl/ (Plug), munal3d bl; *Back:* **Alamy Stock Photo:** funkyfood London - Paul Williams cr; **Dreamstime.com:** All Music Instruments Photos tl, Anton Starikov ftl, Ilya Zaytsev bc; **Getty Images:** Tom Szczerbowski tc; **Getty Images / iStock:** Sunshower Shots br; **Science Photo Library:** Dirk Wiersma cra; **TurboSquid:** CREO with Chris bl; *Spine:* **Alamy Stock Photo:** Dinodia Photos RF ca, Science Photo Library / Kateryna Kon b; **Dreamstime.com:** Toon Sang cb; **Shutterstock.com:** Sebastian Janicki t